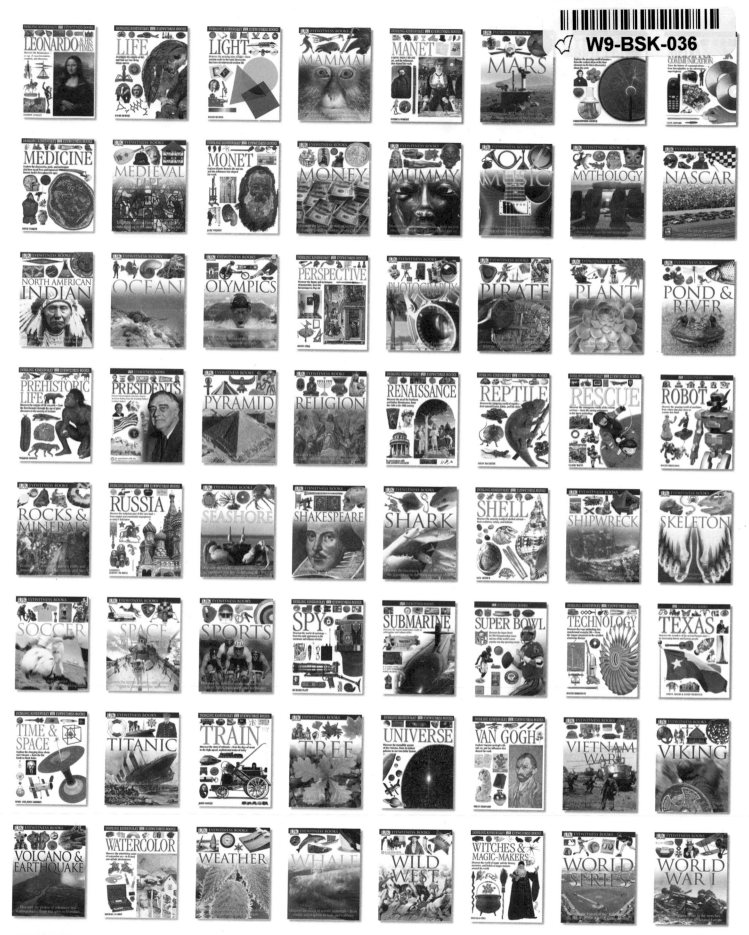

ARCHEOLOGY

Small brush

Measuring tape

Iron slave manacles from Roman Britain, 1st–2nd century A.D.

Sample of peat

Half-restored bronze bowl, United Arab Emirates, 1st century A.D.

Bronze manicure set from Roman London, 2nd century A.D.

Stone mold with bronze chisel and large flat ax

Lion perfume vase from Etruscan Italy, c. 300 B.C.

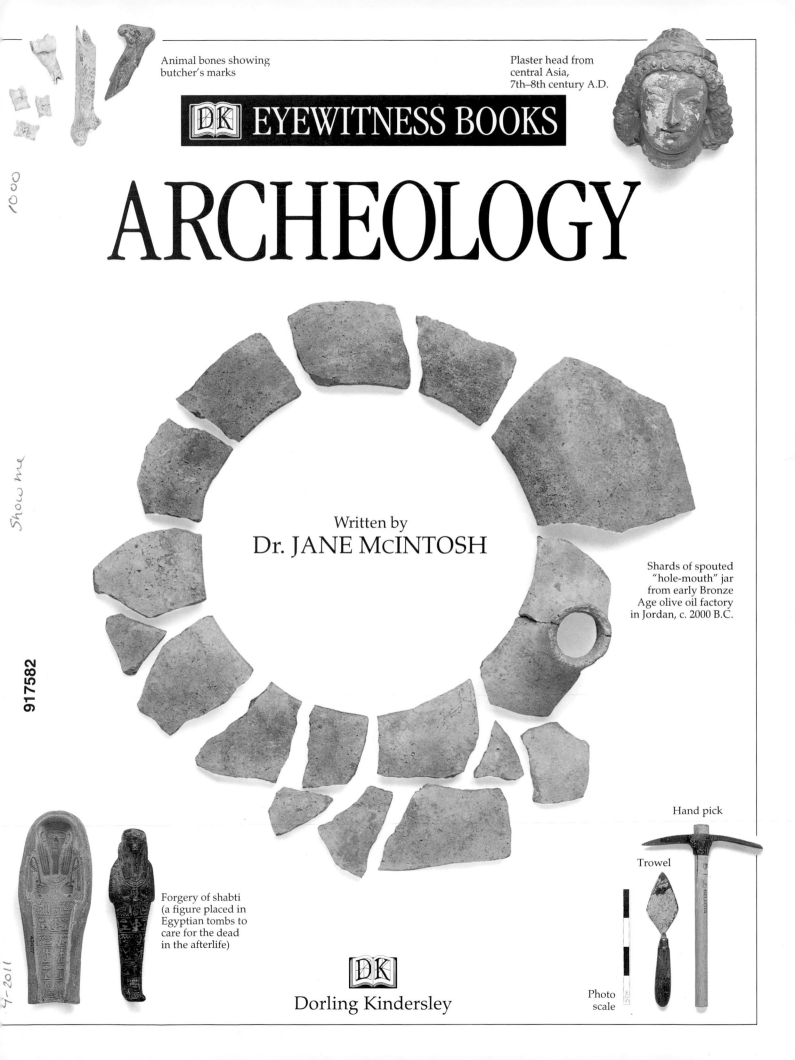

Animal bones showing butcher's marks

Plaster head from central Asia, 7th–8th century A.D.

DK EYEWITNESS BOOKS

ARCHEOLOGY

Written by
Dr. JANE McINTOSH

Shards of spouted "hole-mouth" jar from early Bronze Age olive oil factory in Jordan, c. 2000 B.C.

Hand pick

Trowel

Forgery of shabti (a figure placed in Egyptian tombs to care for the dead in the afterlife)

Photo scale

DK
Dorling Kindersley

917582

Cast-iron hands, an example of industrial archeology

Dorling Kindersley

LONDON, NEW YORK, AUCKLAND, DELHI,
JOHANNESBURG, MUNICH, PARIS and SYDNEY

For a full catalog, visit

www.dk.com

Project editor Marion Dent
Art editor Vicky Wharton
Managing editor Simon Adams
Managing art editor Julia Harris
Research Céline Carez
Picture research Miriam Sharland
Production Catherine Semark
Special photography Geoff Brightling

This Eyewitness ® Book has been conceived by
Dorling Kindersley Limited and Editions Gallimard

Library of Congress Cataloging-in-Publication Data
McIntosh, Jane.
Archeology / written by Jane McIntosh.
p. cm. — (Eyewitness Books)
1. Archaeology—Juvenile literature. [1. Archaeology.] I. Title.
CC171.M36 2000 930.1—dc20 94-9378
ISBN 0-7894-5865-9 (pb)
ISBN 0-7894-5864-0 (hc)

Color reproduction by Colourscan, Singapore
Printed in China by Toppan Printing Co. (Shenzhen) Ltd.

Twentieth-century copy of a
Visigothic gold eagle brooch
of the 6th century A.D.

Roman *amphora*
for storing olive oil

Three coins (
Roman empero
Claudius – rea
contemporar
forgery, an
modern forger

Plaster head,
5th century A.D.,
found in deserts
of central Asia

Black-glazed
drinking vessel
from Etruscan Italy,
4th century B.C.

Contents

Bronze
caldron from
Sutton Hoo

Detecting the past

WHAT IS ARCHEOLOGY? The actual word comes from the Greek and means "the study of what is ancient." It is the past seen from a human perspective. Archeologists, paleontologists, and historians are all interested in the past, but their viewpoints are different. Paleontologists study fossilized remains, while historians deal with written records – the "conscious" past. For archeologists, fossil and documentary findings are only two of many sources of information. Archeologists deal with all the information we can obtain about the past from material remains – evidence that is generally biased and incomplete, but whose scope is almost unlimited.

"Lucy," an unusually complete fossil skeleton of Australopithecus afarensis, *the earliest species directly ancestral to us*

Sacrum (connecting spine to pelvis)

Female pelvis

Details of Lucy's skeleton, such as a thigh bone, show that she walked upright

"YOU CAN'T TAKE IT WITH YOU"
Many past societies believed that you could, and buried the dead with everything they would need in the afterlife. This fluted, Byzantine silver bowl from the Sutton Hoo burial illustrates all that is spectacular in archeology. Made in the Eastern Mediterranean, it found its way to England and was deliberately placed as a funerary offering in the rich ship burial of a king (pp. 26–27). Valuable, exotic, luxurious objects like this reflect not only the status of the owner, but also the trading patterns of a society, its prosperity, and its beliefs.

HOW OLD IS THE HUMAN RACE?
This has been a burning question since Charles Darwin's *Origin of Species* (1859) introduced the concept of evolution. Discovering the remains of our earliest ancestors takes both inspired choice of dig sites and good luck. Hominids (human ancestral species) like Lucy were not numerous. Major geological changes or natural disasters such as volcanoes and earthquakes had to occur before the few fossilized remains were exposed.

SURPRISE!
Archeologists are interested in every aspect of life. It is surprising how much information, particularly about diet and health, can be gained from toilets, like this one from the Viking era in York, England. People accidentally drop things in, but rarely retrieve them! Ancient garbage is invaluable in reconstructing people's lives.

Preserved oak leaf from the Mary Rose *(pp. 32-35)*

LIVING IN THE PAST
Today archeologists are interested in the whole way of life of people in the past, including the landscape that they inhabited. Plant remains, from charred grains and pollen to this oak leaf from the *Mary Rose*, provide evidence of past vegetation. This is supplemented by clues from snails and other minibeasts. Now we can begin to see not only what the world looked like in the past, but also how people have changed it.

Face is off-center, showing how carelessly bowl was crafted

CHILDREN'S PLAYTHINGS
Much of the excitement of the past lies in its rich diversity, but it is also fascinating to see how similar people are from age to age. These two rag dolls were made 2000 years apart, but the children who owned them must have had many feelings and games in common.

Much-loved rag doll from Roman-occupied Egypt, early A.D.

Rag doll "Columbia" from 1890s U.S.

Leather sandals, Britain, 2nd century A.D.

A STEP BACK IN TIME
Most material from which archeologists reconstruct the past was preserved by accident – for example, when a house collapsed, preserving all contents in their places. More commonly, archeologists find house foundations with rubbish thrown into nearby garbage pits, or objects accidentally lost by ancient owners, or inorganic materials (pottery and stone tools), but occasionally organic remains like clothing survive.

Silver bowl – a rich offering in grave of Raedwald, High King of England, c. A.D. 625

STANDING STONES
The most striking ancient remains are monuments, such as England's Stonehenge (left) or Mexico's Olmec heads (pp. 12–13). But how were they built and why? We may gain some understanding of the technology and manpower used to erect such monuments, but the "why" may baffle us forever.

Preservation and decay

LITTLE OF THE PAST ENDURES. Only a fraction of the things used in a person's lifetime ends up in the ground – objects that are lost, thrown away, or deliberately buried. Of these, only a few survive. Some decay naturally, others are physically destroyed, and the chances of survival decrease as time passes. Of those few intact objects, only a very small proportion is likely to be rediscovered and even less of what is uncovered is properly recorded and preserved. It is from this tiny fraction that archeologists attempt to reconstruct the past. This means that we know a great deal more about some aspects of life than others.

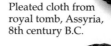

Pleated cloth from royal tomb, Assyria, 8th century B.C.

X-ray examination showed gold beads within cloth

MAKING AN IMPRESSION .
Textiles and other organic materials only survive in exceptional conditions. Sometimes they survive as impressions on objects or in soil, as this cloth did, but ancient clothing is mainly known from art.

MADE OF METAL
Ancient gold and silver survive well, but copper and bronze can suffer surface corrosion. Iron rusts, and may be completely destroyed. Scientific examination of shapeless metal lumps reveals the original appearance, which may be restored by conservation.

BUILDING MATERIALS
Usually wooden buildings survive only as postholes. Durable building stone was often robbed for reuse. Mounds developed where successive brick structures were leveled and new ones built. Abandoned stone or brick settlements, like Pakistan's great 4000-year-old Mohenjo-daro, have often survived.

Iron socketed ax, Britain, c. 7th–6th century B.C.

BOTTOMS UP!
Pottery is about the most common find from archeological sites worldwide from the last 10,000 years. Although it is easily broken, there are few environments where broken pieces will not survive indefinitely. Vessels made of other materials are much less commonly found. Usually they were less durable, and often more expensive, so they were treasured and in shorter supply. Glass degenerates in many soils, while containers of leather, wood, or plant materials rarely survive.

Lotus flower design

One of the earliest examples of Roman blown glass, 1st century A.D.

Lotus cup from Egypt, c. 1250 B.C., made of faience, a type of glazed pottery

Simple red-ware pottery bowl from the Neolithic (Ukraine, 3700–3000 B.C.)

Skull, from Herculaneum in Italy, preserved in ash

Leather lace on either side to tie bikini – like some modern designs

BARELY DECENT

Fashions do not always change with the passing of time – this modern-looking leather bikini bottom is nearly 2000 years old! It has survived because it wound up in a timber-lined well in Roman London, where waterlogging prevented its decay. Wells are a rich source of organic remains of all kinds. So, too, are dry environments such as caves in highland Mexico or the pueblos of the Southwest.

HEADHUNTING

The survival of human remains is very variable. Many soils preserve bones, so skeletons are the most common find, but in acid peat bogs bones may disappear while skin, hair, and insides survive. The body may completely disappear and still be detectable – like Sutton Hoo sand bodies (pp. 42–43) or Pompeii's lava molds (pp. 28–29). In completely arid environments dried bodies are found, while "deep freeze" conditions can ensure perfect preservation (pp. 30–31).

Ancient Egyptian mummy

Blue glass with thin threads of white glass decoration

Drinking horn from kingdom of the Lombards, northern Italy, 6th century A.D.

Stave-built vessel for holding liquids – made from narrow pieces of wood encircled by wooden bands

Wooden drinking vessel used by a soldier or sailor aboard the *Mary Rose*, which sank in 1545

Underground

How does the past get under the ground? The ground level gradually rises over the years, burying the past beneath it. Layer upon layer of decaying vegetation, soil eroded from rocks and hills by weather and rivers, pieces of demolished buildings, even garbage thrown down on the street – all pile up in horizontal layers, the oldest layers at the bottom, the most recent at the top. These may be disturbed by natural disasters such as earthquakes, or by people digging holes. The process of horizontal deposition, known as stratification, is vital in dating the past.

BLOWOUT
Volcanic eruptions dramatically bury the past. The eruption of Santorini in the Aegean Sea, c. 1500 B.C., completely blew out the center of the island, burying beautifully painted Minoan houses under volcanic deposits.

SQUALID DWELLINGS
Layers of deposits develop rapidly in towns. The earth floors of these houses in England's Viking York (Jorvik) rose as mud was brought in on shoes, and debris was thrown on the floor. The wattle-walled houses of woven sticks were often repaired or rebuilt, always at a slightly higher level to match the constantly rising street level.

Roman pit cut away by medieval pit

WELL-FLATTENED
The way deposits accumulate depends partly on how the remains decay. The Sutton Hoo ship burial (pp. 26–27) was covered in sand, preserving details of its decayed timbers. But in the central wooden chamber, sand was kept out until the roof collapsed, by which time many objects had decayed. Those remaining were scattered by the roof fall, and many were crushed.

Part of a superb sheet bronze caldron crushed flat when the roof collapsed

A SLICE THROUGH TIME
A section through part of the 2000-year-old city of London illustrates the constant rise in urban levels through time. The ground level at various periods can be established by looking at floors. From these levels, features were dug – mostly cesspits – which cut through earlier floor levels and deposits. Between floors, debris accumulated in subsequent years, or was deliberately shoveled in to level the ground before rebuilding. The rate of development accelerated in recent centuries.

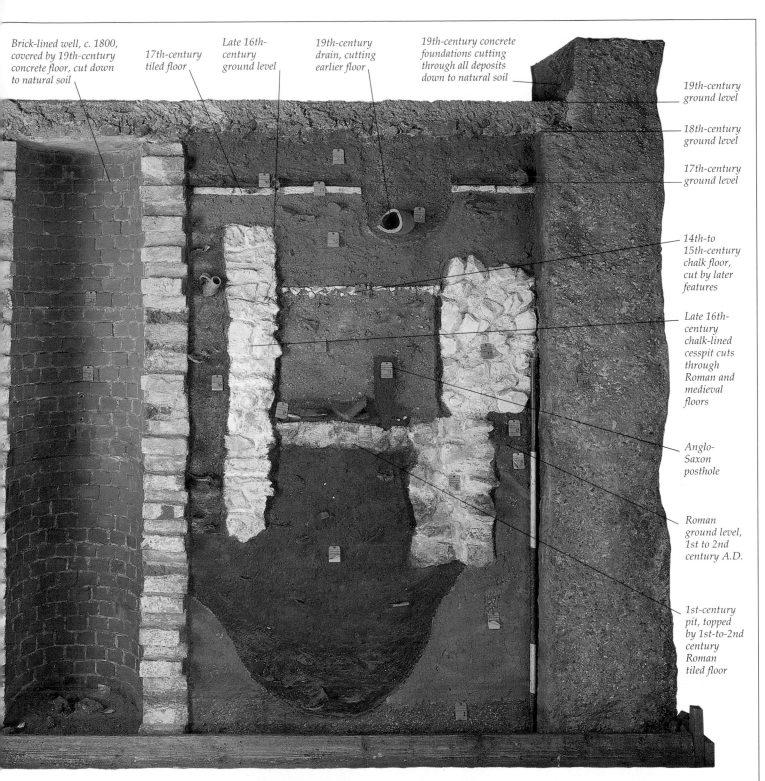

Brick-lined well, c. 1800, covered by 19th-century concrete floor, cut down to natural soil

17th-century tiled floor

Late 16th-century ground level

19th-century drain, cutting earlier floor

19th-century concrete foundations cutting through all deposits down to natural soil

19th-century ground level

18th-century ground level

17th-century ground level

14th-to 15th-century chalk floor, cut by later features

Late 16th-century chalk-lined cesspit cuts through Roman and medieval floors

Anglo-Saxon posthole

Roman ground level, 1st to 2nd century A.D.

1st-century pit, topped by 1st-to-2nd century Roman tiled floor

SIX FEET UNDER

Usually the past gets underground by accident, but sometimes people deliberately bury valuables during troubled times, or in human burials. Some graves are simple, others elaborate tombs. The tomb of Egyptian pharaoh Tutankhamun survived the usual ancient tomb robbing, to be dramatically rediscovered by Howard Carter in 1922.

BRAVING THE ELEMENT

Intrepid explorers John Lloyd Stephens and Frederick Catherwood rediscovered the Maya civilization in inhospitable jungle. Lush vegetation, numerous insects, and tropical climate make jungles rapid destroyers of antiquities, but also protect against looters.

Looking at the landscape

MODERN ARCHEOLOGISTS look at the whole landscape used by humans – ancient dwellings, fields, and woodlands associated with settlements or land that shows traces of early people's activities. Survey methods used to investigate these large areas are cheap and rapid, unlike excavations. But not everything that lies under the ground can be detected from above. Aerial reconnaisance, remote sensing, and geophysical survey can detect some things better than others, so they show only a partial picture of what lies under the ground. Material, such as pottery shards or brick, scattered on the surface may indicate buried features that are being disturbed, particularly by plowing. But only recent features, lying close to the ground's surface, are the most likely to produce such evidence, while earlier ones may remain undisturbed.

LYING AROUND
You do not need to dig to discover the past. Field walking involves the systematic collection, recording, and mapping of material lying on the surface. It allows settlements and other buried activity areas to be identified and dated.

"MOON BUGGY"
Geophysical survey equipment, using radar, echo-sounding, electrical resistivity, or magnetic variation, picks up variations in the soil that reflect buried features. Different machines can "see" to different depths and detect different things. However, their results must be interpreted carefully.

Modern field boundary

Winter wheat ripens faster, and is paler, over buried ditches

Modern pipeline trench

Now-dry watercourse flowed in Roman times

Roman linear settlement – ditches acted like garden fences around Roman buildings

Modern ditch

Modern track follows line of medieval track, dividing blocks of medieval fields

Perimeter of Iron-Age enclosure, with ditch and internal bank

Recently dug stream

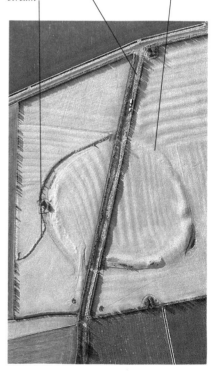

SNAKING ACROSS THE LANDSCAPE
Enduring structures such as mounds are the surviving stubs of ancient landscapes.The Serpent Mound in Ohio (above) was a religious monument built by the Adena people who began building mounds in what is now southern Ohio, c. 700 B.C. It is a visible relic of a landscape that originally included burials and villages.

CROP MARKS FROM THE AIR
The vital water available to growing plants is reduced by such buried obstructions as walls and increased by buried holes, such as ditches. Plants germinate sooner, grow taller, and ripen earlier over buried holes. The patterns of these differences in growth are clearly visible from the air. This photo shows a Roman peat-cutting settlement in the wet fenlands of eastern England; ovals (bottom right) are modern tractor marks.

AN AERIAL VIEW OF SHADOW SITES
When the sun is low, even slight variations in the ground's surface cast clear shadows best seen from the air – like a patterned carpet seen by a person instead of a mouse. Spotting patterns is only the beginning – skill and experience are needed to interpret them. Above is an Iron-Age hillfort in eastern England. The horizontal and vertical lines show where strip fields once were; the circles (bottom left) are modern horse troughs.

Helmets, such as this, may have been worn to protect players in Central America's ritual ball game

Basalt blocks were used for these heads and weighed as much as 34 tons

Typical Olmec features

BIG BROTHER IS WATCHING
Colossal heads of basalt are an outstanding creation of the Olmec people (1200–600 B.C.) of Mexico's eastern coast. Heads like the one above were deliberately mutilated and buried and may be portraits of rulers. The Olmecs owed their prosperity to rich soils capable of producing two crops a year. The Olmec people dominated the long-distance trade network that flourished throughout Central America and initiated such typical features as advanced astronomy and a complicated calender.

HILLS AND HOLES
Abandoned sites that have not been rebuilt can often be mapped directly. Bumps and hollows may be visible on the surface of the ground, even under vegetation. They give a clear plan of features that once stood there, which can be identified by their similarities to other excavation sites. Laguna de los Cerros' undulating pastures (left) cover typical features of Olmec ceremonial centers – pyramids, plazas, platforms, and ball courts.

All kinds of documents

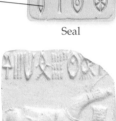

DOCUMENTS – inscriptions, coins, maps, official records, or letters, for example – help us to understand the past. They contain information that may not exist elsewhere and give us direct access to what earlier peoples thought. But it is for this very reason that we must be wary. Writing always has a purpose, which means it can be biased. Not all documents are in writing, though. Maps may be purely visual and important historical material can be conveyed in traditional tales. Place names and language also provide invaluable records.

MAN WITH A DREAM
Oral records are valuable. In the 8th century B.C., Homer wrote the *Iliad*, looking back 400 years to a vanished, but not forgotten, world. Following Homer's clues, Heinrich Schliemann set out to discover Troy in the 1870s (above) – and unexpectedly succeeded.

Inscription too short to give good clues for deciphering

Seal

Impression

Impression

Seal

Bull seal

Bull impression

Inscription revealed by infra-red photography

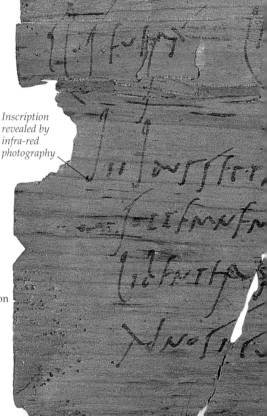

PUZZLE OF THE INDUS CIVILIZATION
Writing reveals a great deal, so it is tantalizing when we cannot read it. Earliest writing of ancient India and Pakistan may never be deciphered, although scholars have identified its language and found its writing goes from right to left. Seals, with picture and brief inscription, were used on merchandise.

FORESEEING THE FUTURE
Writing began to meet one of two needs – to keep official records, as in Sumer (now southern Iraq), or to deal with religious matters. In China questions to the gods were written on bones (above) which were heated. This caused cracks whose pattern was interpreted to give answers.

1450 map of Constantinople

FINDING ONE'S WAY AROUND
Archeological studies of towns or countrysides are likely to start with maps. Place names reveal vanished features and the history of local settlement. Anomalies, or irregularities, such as bends in hedge lines or street layouts may show where features such as mounds or city walls have disappeared. But old maps, like other documents, may be biased. They provide information for a purpose – what is not relevant may be left out. Great care is needed when interpreting them.

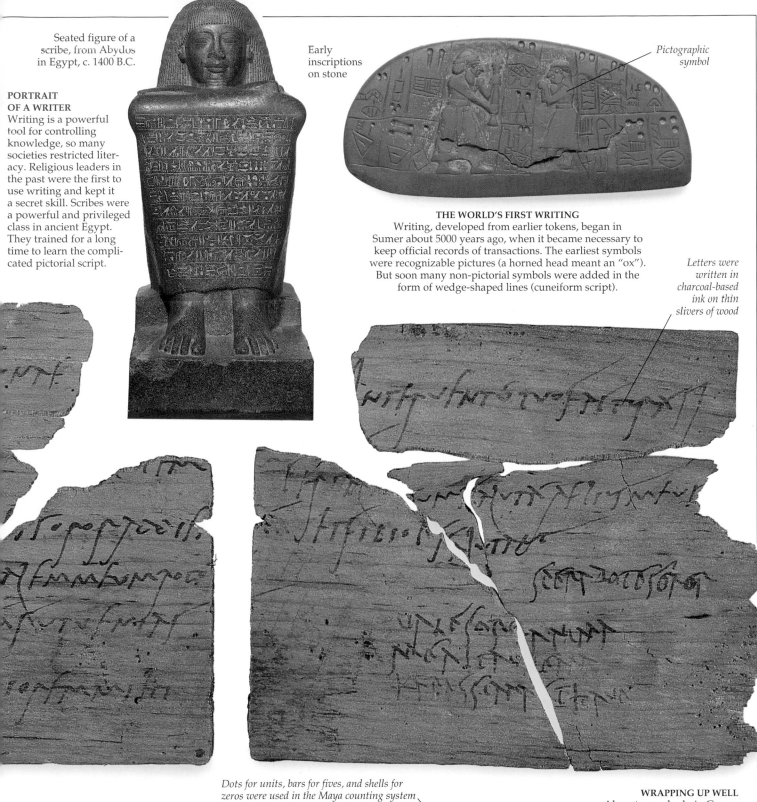

**PORTRAIT
OF A WRITER**
Writing is a powerful
tool for controlling
knowledge, so many
societies restricted liter-
acy. Religious leaders in
the past were the first to
use writing and kept it
a secret skill. Scribes were
a powerful and privileged
class in ancient Egypt.
They trained for a long
time to learn the compli-
cated pictorial script.

Seated figure of a
scribe, from Abydos
in Egypt, c. 1400 B.C.

Early
inscriptions
on stone

*Pictographic
symbol*

THE WORLD'S FIRST WRITING
Writing, developed from earlier tokens, began in
Sumer about 5000 years ago, when it became necessary to
keep official records of transactions. The earliest symbols
were recognizable pictures (a horned head meant an "ox").
But soon many non-pictorial symbols were added in the
form of wedge-shaped lines (cuneiform script).

*Letters were
written in
charcoal-based
ink on thin
slivers of wood*

MAYA CODEX
The Maya (c. A.D. 300–900)
were among the world's
greatest mathematicians and
astronomers. Their methods of
recording dates were extremely
complex. They used both a 52-
year repeating cycle and histori-
ical dates starting from August
13, 3113 B.C. Although many of
their texts, like this codex, are
religious, stelae (inscribed
stone pillars) tell of political
organization and the warlike
activities of their rulers.

*Dots for units, bars for fives, and shells for
zeros were used in the Maya counting system*

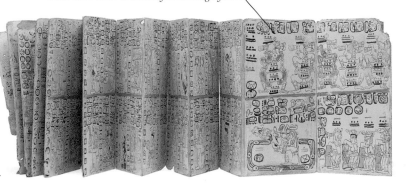

WRAPPING UP WELL
Almost everybody in Greece
and Rome could read and
write, as shown by the wonderful discovery of letters in
the Roman military outpost
at Vindolanda in northern
England. These range from
official military records of
stores to chatty correspondence
sent to the garrison. One lists
winter clothes being sent to a
chilly soldier – two pairs of
sandals, some wool socks,
and two pairs of underpants!

Images of the past

ART IS NOT ONLY ATTRACTIVE, it is also a window into the past. Paintings and sculptures can show objects such as clothing or wooden architecture that have survived in archeological sites only as fragments or not at all. Detailed scenes of everyday life, as in ancient Egyptian paintings, show how people lived and how they carried out their work. But art is often symbolic and has a deeper meaning for its creators. Australian Aborigine paintings depict their mythology, which we cannot understand without their explanations. Without written or verbal information to provide a key, it is hard to unlock the meaning of art.

BUSHMEN'S ROCK ART
Southern Africa's paintings and rock engravings are largely naturalistic, depicting people and animals. Many provide detailed information on hunting practices and equipment. Most of this art is relatively recent, while that of Australia's Aborigines has a much longer history. Nevertheless, both form part of a living tradition, telling stories of the universe and its creation.

Mythology and ritual are embodied in Australia's Aborigine art. The act of repainting can be an integral part of ritual activity.

THE BEAUTY OF INDIAN ART
The period from the 2nd century B.C. to the 3rd century A.D. saw the finest flowering of Buddhist art in India, at its peak in the sculptures associated with "stupas" (mounds covering venerated Buddhist cremated remains). Their erection reflects not only religious fervor, but also political and economic prosperity. The Amaravati stupa (three slabs of it shown) is perhaps the finest. Although the subject matter is religious, the art style has its roots in long-established folk traditions.

Hairstyles and furnishings are shown in great detail – on the left a group of musicians play clearly identifiable instruments

This roundel decorated a crossbar on the stupa railing – it shows a scene of courtly life, illustrating a story of one of the Buddha's past lives

THE PROBLEMS OF DATING
Dating rock art poses a problem. One clue is similarities in style between rock art and other, dateable artwork. Another is the depiction of artifacts whose dates are known – such as the Bronze-Age tools and weapons in this Swedish rock painting. The different kinds of boats illustrated also help establish the valuable information on seafaring. Other contemporary Bronze-Age rock art in Europe shows aspects of agriculture, such as plowing with oxen.

Elephant, wheel, and horse are symbols that allow us to identify the main figure here as the Chakravartin – the Universal Monarch

Buddha's renunciation of his princely life

Tiered umbrellas on the summit of stupas symbolize royalty

Birth of the Buddha

Queen Maya's dream of Buddha's conception

Some stupa carvings show many decorative elements on the upper portion of the dome

Surviving slabs from the otherwise completely destroyed stupa depict similar stupas, giving us a clear picture of its original appearance

Other carvings depict lavish flower garlands

Seated lions guard the gateway

Worshipers surround the stupa

The stupa was surrounded by a stone railing, its outer face decorated with lotus roundels

Buddha with worshippers

A COBBLER'S TALE
Even though art is often symbolic or has a deeper meaning, it can give excellent detailed information about the daily life of its creators. Greek painted pottery often depicts mythological subjects, but it also shows us many aspects of Greek life. Here a cobbler is cutting and shaping strips of leather – above him hang finished sandals, boots, and the tools of his trade. By closely examining stylistic details, scholars have been able to identify the work of individual painters – some even signed their artwork.

Viking warrior burials contained weapons but no armor, so artwork like this provides valuable information

THE WALRUS AND ITS IVORY
The walrus-ivory chessmen from Scotland's Isle of Lewis depict Viking society. The pawns are foot soldiers, while the knights, bishops, kings, and queens represent the upper classes in the social hierarchy. This knight shows his expensive warrior equipment – horse and trappings, including stirrups, which were a recent innovation.

Walking among the past

MUCH OF A TOWN'S PAST can be discovered just by looking at it carefully, for the layout of original settlements influences later construction. When old buildings are torn down, the shape of the empty space is echoed by new constructions. Curved streets may mark where a town wall, now long vanished, once stood. The architectural styles of houses and the organization of streets differ greatly throughout the ages. Buildings may survive, but in modified forms – old houses divided into apartments, tiny cottages joined together. Architectural details can reveal individual structures' history, while place names can tell of vanished features, activities, or inhabitants.

SECOND THOUGHTS
Cordoba's mosque was extended for a second time in A.D. 987, its earlier outer wall becoming part of the interior. Building alterations are valuable clues for reconstructing history.

THE *MIHRAB*
This new *mihrab* (sacred niche) was built when Cordoba's mosque was extended in A.D. 961. Although clearly related in design to earlier parts, this and other elements of the extension are more imaginative and their decoration much richer.

Mihrab was the mosque's focal point of worship

Typical Arab feature

Horseshoe arch, typical of southern Spain, is derived from Visigothic architecture

CHRISTIAN VANDALISM
In 1236, Cordoba was reconquered by the Christian rulers of Spain, and the mosque was altered to become a church. But in the 1500s, the entire center was destroyed to build an ornate cathedral. The gaudy decoration of its dome contrasts with the Muslim *mihrab*'s restrained beauty.

THE DOOR TO MAGNIFICENCE
The Visigoths (Germanic tribes) seized Cordoba from the Romans, but later lost it to the Arabs. Little survives from the Visigothic period (c. A.D. 500–719), but their church was the basis for the mosque built here in A.D. 786. St. Stephen's Gate, the oldest remaining entrance to the mosque, was built into surviving walls.

Roman pillar survived to become part of the later structure

ROME STANDS FOREVER
Several major modern streets of the Spanish town of Cordoba, with Roman milestones, still follow the Roman layout. Portions of the wall remain, indicating the town's original extent. Many pillars show where impressive Roman buildings once stood (left).

ON HIGH
Cordoba's cathedral dominates the mosque. Around it, narrow streets preserve a portion of the medieval city – its Jewish quarter (Juderia), whose name records its former inhabitants. Bounding this is part of the Roman city wall, a legible historical document showing its original construction, Arab additions, reconquest damage, and later rebuilding.

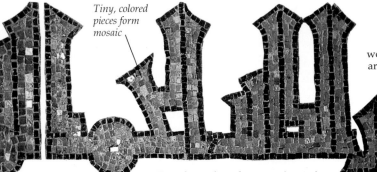

Tiny, colored
pieces form
mosaic

*Calligraphy and flowers
decorate Muslim architecture –
showing people and animals is
prohibited by Islamic religion*

INSIDE THE MOSQUE

The construction of the great
mosque at Cordoba reused Roman
and Visigothic pillars from an earlier
church, but significantly altered both
its layout and its structure. By
the addition of stone pillars and
arches above the earlier columns,
the original restricted church was
transformed into a tall, light,
spacious structure.

SUPERB CALLIGRAPHY
Among the lavish but
restrained decoration of the
wonderful 10th-century *mihrab*
are lines of ornate calligraphy.
This is used for decorative
effect as well as to display
verses from the Koran
(Muslim holy book).
Al-Hakam II (the ruler
who commissioned the
mihrab) is mentioned.

*Horseshoe arches echo mosque's exterior,
with alternating brick and stone*

*Shortened
pyramid
added above
column
supports
massive
stone pillar*

*Details
show how
Roman and
Visigothic
column
capitals
differ*

*Extensions
to the
mosque can
be identified
from such
details as
variations in
the styles
of arches*

*Roman and Visigothic
columns and capitals were reused*

Why excavate?

From the 14th century on, collectors sought ancient artifacts. They hoped these would increase their knowledge of the past, which was based only on ancient texts. By the 1800s, the treasure hunt had led to the discovery of great lost civilizations. Advances in geological studies suggested that these cultures were incredibly old, but dating the artifacts was a problem.

Extensive digging, at different strata, or layers, in the soil was done in order to develop chronological sequences. Today, scientific dating has freed modern excavators from this need – however, it also means there is little justification for the massive treasure hunting of the past.

A LEISURELY INTEREST
Demands for artifacts created a tomb-robbing industry, which still continues. Etruscan tombs, with their fine frescoes and reliefs, were a sight on the Grand Tour of Europe in the 1700s.

Superb, black-glazed *rhyton* (drinking vessel) from the François tomb at Vulci, Italy

UNCOVERING THE TRUTH?
The François tomb contained many wonderful artifacts, such as this drinking vessel. A fresco in the tomb showed a well-known episode from Roman history, but it illustrated a quite different Etruscan version, thereby casting doubts on the Roman account. An important conclusion was drawn – that archeology could contribute to knowledge in its own right, rather than merely illustrating history.

A well-to-do lady from ancient Clusium, shown lying on the lid of her sarcophagus and holding a mirror

Mirror, 300–200 B.C., is inscribed "Grave gift of Suthina"

VANDALISM ON A LARGE SCALE
The 19th century saw the rediscovery of great civilizations. Spectacular architecture and sculpture (palaces, tombs, and temples) attracted most attention. National pride played a shameful role in excavation. Here at Nineveh in Iraq, French and British teams competed to carry off monumental remains to adorn their own national museums.

REFLECTIONS OF ANTIQUITY
Intricately engraved bronze mirrors were among the most beautiful of Etruscan objects. In the late 1800s, catalogs (such as ones devoted to Etruscan mirrors) helped scholars reconstruct the history of the shadowy Etruscans, great traders from North Italy.

ETRUSCAN PLACES
Excavation methods in the mid-1800s were still in their infancy. Though systematic recording of finds was growing, the emphasis was still on retrieving objects from prominent sites, such as these Etruscan tombs at Orvieto in central Italy, despite hordes of mosquitoes and bandits. Etruscan remains provided a patriotic ancestry for the newly unified Italian nation.

Gold wreath
of ivy leaves,
c. 300–200 B.C.

Exquisite gold
earrings,
c. 350–300 B.C.

ALL THAT GLITTERS
At first, excavators collected beautiful and valuable objects for their own sake, but later they sought artifacts that were distinctive and would contribute to our knowledge of the past. Modern excavators actively seek the more mundane artifacts their predecessors threw away, for they can tell us as much, if not more, about how life was lived in the past.

GREECE IN ITALY
In the early 1900s, many archeologists believed that European culture developed from the civilizations of western Asia and Greece. Etruscans, whose frescoes depicted Greek legends, were thought to come from eastern Greece. More recent excavations proved that Etruscan culture developed locally. It was trade that made Greek things fashionable.

RESTING IN PEACE
Excavations of the 1800s concentrated on tombs, yielding fine pottery and sarcophagii (coffins). Recognizing style changes became an archeological preoccupation. By arranging the artifacts in sequence, the stylistic changes provided a rough dating system.

Useful mortar unearthed by excavation of Etruscan settlement

EXCAVATION NOW
Preoccupation with the great and glorious continued well into the 20th century. But today excavation is done both to save the past from destruction and to answer particular questions. Field investigations followed by site excavations answer questions about the daily lives, industry, religion, and politics of the Etruscans.

Painted sarcophagus, 300–150 B.C., is well within the Roman period, but it still follows Etruscan traditions

Digging up the past

ARCHEOLOGISTS excavate "sites." This elastic term can cover a blind for hunting or a complete town. During excavation a site is carefully taken apart in the reverse order to how it was formed. The topsoil is removed first to reveal "features," which are anomalies created by people such as pits or postholes, walls, roads, or yards. Archeologists then look also for "layers," distinct deposits of soil that show differences in the way they were formed, due to environmental factors or human activities. One of an archeologist's chief skills must be the ability to detect variations in soil, such as color, texture, and feel.

Dental picks for fine work and fragile remains

Photo scale indicates size of small objects in photos

Small brush to clean away grains of loose soil around objects

33-ft cloth tape for general site recording – laying out the site, planning, and section drawing

Plumb bob for correct vertical plotting

5Cm

TOOLS FOR THE JOB
After removal of vegetation and topsoil, the area is cleared to reveal the uppermost archeological features. These are investigated individually, using small picks or trowels. Loose soil is removed with a hand shovel and trowel or brush, but delicate objects may require dental picks, teaspoons, and tiny brushes. Recording is absolutely vital, so archeologists also have measuring and drawing equipment. Wheelbarrows and buckets remove soil to the dump – and provide seats at coffee breaks!

LAYING OUT THE SITE
At the start of an excavation, a fixed point is established, of known height above or below sea level. This is the point to which the height of all measurements on site will be related. A fixed base line is set up and its position mapped. All subsequent horizontal points, including the trenches to be excavated, are worked out in relation to this. During excavation surveying equipment records the heights of different layers and finds.

ENTRENCHED VIEW
Before an excavation begins, the site director must decide where to start digging, then plan and recruit the people needed to carry out the work – experienced supervisors, specialists, and diggers (often students or local laborers). Permission for the excavation to start, as well as funding for the cost of excavation, must be obtained. Once everything is ready, the parts of the site to be excavated are marked out, often in squares or rectangles. Shown above is a model of the site of Tell es-Sa'idiyeh in Jordan at the end of the 1993 season.

LIFE'S UPS AND DOWNS
Remains can be found at three levels – aboveground, at ground level, and belowground. So when a site is excavated, archeologists will first encounter remains of walls sticking up into the topsoil. From these, excavators can make a plan of contemporary structures, which are then individually excavated down to their ground level, followed by their pits and other holes belowground. In this step-by-step manner, the site is taken apart, from present to past.

SOGGY SLOGGING
This brushwood trackway in England's Somerset Levels contrasts strongly with the excavation in Jordan. The wetland site has soggy digging conditions and waterlogged finds. A plastic shelter keeps rain off diggers and, more important, prevents the sun from drying out the waterlogged road. The peat is peeled away with Popsicle sticks and plastic spatulas. Toe boards lessen pressure on wood below the surface. Despite differences, all excavations share the same basic principles, aims, and hard work!

Bricklayer's
pointing trowel,
the all-
purpose
tool

Hand pick, the most
widely used digging
tool in the Near East

*Position of
every object
and bone is
recorded*

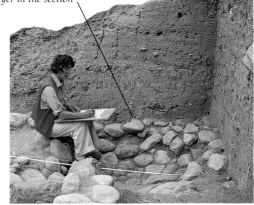

CARE OF THE DEAD
Excavating a burial is a delicate
operation involving fine dental
tools, brushes, and trowels. Grave
goods can include tiny objects, such
as beads, so great care is exercised.
Often all soil from the grave pit is
sieved to recover any item that
has been overlooked.

A GRAVE SITUATION
Usually burials are in a
grave, dug from the ground
surface of a particular period.
Inside this may be a coffin or
a jar, containing a skeleton
(left), with its grave goods.
The bronze javelin showed
that this burial at Tell es-
Sa'idiyeh was of a warrior –
its corrosion has preserved
mineralized traces of linen,
indicating that the person
had been tightly bound.

*Label identifies individual
layer in the section*

COMMITTED TO PAPER
Detailed recording is an absolutely vital
part of excavation. As well as photographs and written records, detailed
drawings are made of all features
and deposits. Plans record the
horizontal aspects of the site,
such as arrangements of house
walls or details of grave pits
and their contents. Section
drawings record the vertical
aspects such as the profile
and fills of features like
pits. Everything on an
excavation drawing is
carefully and accurately
recorded to scale.

*These jars were found
with others in a complex
that was probably an
administrative center
for the distribution of
locally-made olive oil*

SIGNIFICANT FINDS
Excavated finds are divided
into two categories – small finds,
and the rest. Small finds are objects
of individual significance, such as grave
goods. What is a small find depends on
what material a site yields. Each small
find is given an individual number, and its
horizontal and vertical position is precisely
recorded. Other things are just finds and are
collected and recorded only by context. The
distinction continues with the processing of
the finds – small finds are carefully cleaned,
perhaps by professional conservators, while
other, less significant finds are often vigorously
cleaned with water and scrubbing brushes.

Two large storage jars from Jordan's
Tell es-Sa'idiyeh – these were
probably used for storing olive oil,
a major export from the area

Things in their place

WHAT DID PEOPLE DO IN THE PAST and why? By themselves, artifacts only tell us what art or utensils were made of in the past and give us a clue to their use. Bones alone have little meaning. Buildings reveal construction methods, and deposits inside, above, or below these features tell us how soil accumulated. But if we put all these pieces together, there is almost unlimited information. Context (where things come from and how they relate to each other) is one of the most important aspects of archeological investigation, which explains why archeologists are so enraged by looting. This takes objects out of context, and destroys our chances of understanding the complete picture.

WHAT'S GOING ON?
What went on in individual rooms of excavated buildings is often clear from objects found inside. Later deposits contain evidence of subsequent activity there.

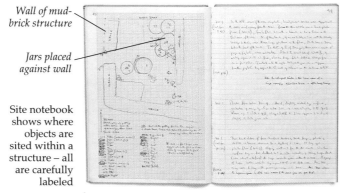

Wall of mud-brick structure

Jars placed against wall

Site notebook shows where objects are sited within a structure – all are carefully labeled

CAPTURED CONTEXT
Many objects are left in their original places within abandoned buildings. Where they were found and what they are may provide information about the building's function. Making detailed plans of these structures and objects in their places is an important part of site recording.

PATTERNS OF ACTIVITY
Remains found together may show a single activity performed in the past. Realtionships between structures within a settlement show how it was organized socially and economically (above). For example, by refitting the pieces knapped (struck) from a piece of flint, the stages in a flint tool's manufacture can be reconstructed. Useless, discarded animal bones found with flint tools may show a butchery site, while meat-bearing bones from the same animal show where people ate.

PACKAGED INFORMATION
Often the objects we find were lost or abandoned, and only preserved by chance. Burials are very special because they contain material deliberately deposited together in the past, in a way that had meaning for the people who made the burial. This means that quite detailed conclusions about society can be drawn from burials.

Crouched position of burials within single or double jars may symbolize a return to the mother's womb

Double jar burial from Tell es-Sa'idiyeh in Jordan

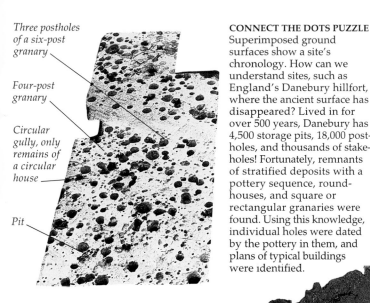

Three postholes of a six-post granary

Four-post granary

Circular gully, only remains of a circular house

Pit

Part of Danebury hillfort, showing a variety of pits and postholes

CONNECT THE DOTS PUZZLE
Superimposed ground surfaces show a site's chronology. How can we understand sites, such as England's Danebury hillfort, where the ancient surface has disappeared? Lived in for over 500 years, Danebury has 4,500 storage pits, 18,000 post-holes, and thousands of stake-holes! Fortunately, remnants of stratified deposits with a pottery sequence, round-houses, and square or rectangular granaries were found. Using this knowledge, individual holes were dated by the pottery in them, and plans of typical buildings were identified.

Pompeii's residents hid in cellars, hoping to escape the blast, but died from poisonous gases

NO ESCAPE!
In the 1800s, visitors to Italy's Herculaneum and Pompeii saw the newly excavated results of Vesuvius's eruption in 79 A.D. They were inspired to create dramatic works of art and literature depicting the lives that had ended so suddenly. Here is one artist's impression of the scene in the wine cellars of a villa at Pompeii (above) where 17 people died in the poses depicted.

Ordinary possessions such as pots were left behind when people fled – these now give important information about everyday life

CAUGHT IN THE ACT
Most things that arche-ologists find were lost, abandoned, or thrown away – such as hairpins or coins dropped acciden-tally, garbage, or things too worn out, too trivial, or too large to be taken when people moved. These items reveal a great deal, but the picture is in-complete. Although burials, hoards, and ritual offerings are deliberately deposited, they only tell us about certain aspects of life. But sudden disasters, such as the asphyxiation of Herculaneum's inhabi-tants (left) by hot ash and gas, are exceptionally informative because they "freeze" existence, allowing us to reconstruct a whole way of life at that moment.

Vegetation will eventually destroy this site at Herculaneum

Mounds and monuments

MOUNDS ARE ARTIFICIAL HILLS designed to dominate the landscape. These and other monuments, built to impress and to attract attention, make a public statement – this is our land, or, our king is the greatest, and so on. The way monuments and mound burials are distributed across the landscape gives important clues to the organization of past societies, as do the burials they may contain. A mound burial may show a ruler's importance, while lesser mortals lie in flat graves. On the other hand, a monument like the European megaliths may cover jumbled skeletal remains of many individuals – an "equal-access" tomb for a more democratic society.

HEAPS OF POWER
Looking at patterns of burial sites provides helpful clues to past social organization. In this 1610 map, the massive burial mounds at England's Sutton Hoo are clearly visible. Recent excavations have revealed many flat graves in the area. It appears to be a cemetery with different social ranks, and the buried grave goods support this.

WORTH HIS WEIGHT IN GOLD
The richness of their grave goods may reflect the status of different individuals. But what was considered valuable in the past? Archeologists think that rare, hard to obtain, or far-traveled materials, or objects that required time or special skill to make, had special value. Sutton Hoo's grave goods, like this gold buckle, were clearly very valuable.

Intricate decoration of interlaced birds and animals

Bronze foil panels decorate the iron helmet

ROW, ROW, ROW THE BOAT
Gold and jeweled belt fittings included the remains of a purse. This contained gold coins, possibly payment for the crew. The date of the most recent coin places the burial no earlier than A.D. 625.

Gold buckle

GHOST SHIP
Meticulous excavations of mounds at Sutton Hoo in the late 1930s revealed Anglo-Saxon remains including a small boat. In the largest mound was a massive ship. All that survived of this 90-ft (27-m) long ship were a hard crust in the sand (the "ghost" of the decayed timbers) and the iron rivets fastening the timbers together. Poorly preserved grave goods, of unprecedented splendor, survived inside a decayed wooden central chamber.

A TOAST TO DEATH
Due to acid soil, the Sutton Hoo metal objects were in pieces and poorly preserved, while bone, horn, textiles, and wood had almost completely vanished. Painstaking recording of the position of every fragment enabled objects to be pieced together and reconstructed.

Reconstructed part

Drinking horn made from a small aurochs

Iron crest had gilded bronze animal heads with garnet eyes

Helmet belonged to King Raedwald, overlord of the English kings, who died in A.D. 625

Carnac alignments may have had some astronomical significance

MYSTERIOUS MONUMENTS

Not all mounds contain burials and not all monuments are mounds. Temples or cathedrals are clearly for religious observances. Other monuments, like these massive ranks of stones dominating the landscape at Carnac in France, are much more enigmatic. Their purpose, hidden now, was obviously very important to their builders. Estimates of the vast amount of labor involved give some idea of the size of the work force needed by their creators.

WARRIOR KING

Archeologists believe that grave goods are chosen to reflect the roles the deceased played in society. So what do the grave goods of Sutton Hoo tell us? Their richness shows their owner's great importance, as does the labor expended in his ship burial and mound. This helmet and weaponry indicate that he was a warrior, a necessity for a leader in warlike Anglo-Saxon society. Objects thought to be a scepter and other royal regalia suggest their owner was a king.

Reconstruction of helmet in 1949

WRONGLY ASSEMBLED

The helmet was found in about 500 small fragments, but only the gilded parts had survived in any recognizable form. Recent doubts about how accurate the first reconstruction was (above), prompted a complete dismantling and a new attempt. It was a painstaking task – putting together a puzzle with most pieces missing and many broken – but a triumph for conservation.

Gilded bronze mouth, nose, and eyebrows formed bird with outstretched wings and gnashing teeth

Hinged neck and ear guards on cap were forged from single piece of iron

Hot and dry

Creature embroidered into fabric

PERFECTLY PRESERVED
The dry coastal regions of Peru have yielded many burials, complete with food, baskets, and colored textiles, perfectly preserved and dried.

ORGANIC REMAINS (those from animals or plants) come from extreme environments like bogs, or polar or desert regions. Microorganisms that cause decay can't live in those cold, dry, or airless situations. Deserts are not easily inhabited by humans, so most of their archeological treasures have come from places with local water supplies, like the Nile in Egypt. Carbonization (burning without oxygen) removes moisture from organic materials, such as carbonized grain, ensuring their survival. More spectacular, but rare, is preservation by volcanic eruptions, which destroy life but preserve death.

A BLAST FROM THE PAST
On August 24, A.D. 79, Mt. Vesuvius erupted, covering the towns of Pompeii in ash and Herculaneum in volcanic mud. Thousands of people were suffocated, and their bodies rapidly covered in ash and pumice, or porous volcanic glass, which cooled to form a solid rock case. Inside these cases, bodies decayed, leaving a mold of their shapes. Pompeii's first serious excavator, Giuseppe Fiorelli, produced plaster casts of these body molds in the 1860s.

Baker's stamp still visible on loaf

BURNED BREAD
Pompeii's streets survive frozen in time, complete with houses, gardens, and shops. Among these are several bakeries, with counters at the front, massive lava milling stones in the back, and bread ovens from which completely carbonized round loaves have been recovered.

Some marks of clothing, pressed tightly against his body by ash and pumice, still visible

Cast of individual sitting out his last moment of life

Grass brush
from central Asia,
7th–8th century A.D.

THE SANDS OF TIME
Centuries ago many prosperous towns, dependent on canal
irrigation for agriculture, were established in the inhospitable
deserts of Central Asia along the Silk Road from China to the
West. Following detailed information in ancient records,
Sir Aurel Stein endured great hardship to trace
these settlements in the early 1900s.

WOODEN CAPITAL (TOP OF THE COLUMN)
Stein uncovered many ancient settlements, their
wooden architecture undecayed, but eroded by
fierce winds. The most important buildings had
beautifully carved wood and stucco decoration,
like this 3rd-century A.D. carved capital.
Official records show an interesting
cultural blend: typical Chinese
wooden tablets but written in
an Indian language and
script, with Western-
style seals.

Roman meals
usually began
with eggs and
ended with
fruit

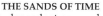

CRACKED EGGS
Many private houses in Pompeii and
Herculaneum still contained domestic
objects in their place – wooden furniture
such as a table and a cot, and wooden
cupboards with pottery and glass vessels.
Some shops had wooden racks supporting
jars full of charred grain and other
scorched food. Tables were laid with
dishes of fruit, nuts, and eggs (above).

HOUSEHOLD GOODS
The houses of ordinary
people in Stein's central Asian
sites contained such well-preserved
domestic artifacts as grass brooms,
wooden chopsticks, felt textiles, and even
mousetraps. Recovering objects from garbage pits,
Stein complained that the smell from these had also
survived the centuries! His most exciting discoveries
were from caves near Tun-Huang in China, where he found
wonderful Buddhist paintings on silk (pp. 50–51) and a vast
library of manuscripts in many different languages and scripts.

Cliff Palace pueblo
at Mesa Verde,
Colorado

VANISHED IN A PUFF OF SMOKE
Dry sites from the New World have
preserved rope sandals, while
hobnails in Roman burials show
their boots were once there.
These leather shoes, minus
their owners, survive in
a carbonized state
in Pompeii.

Carbonized
soles of shoes
from Pompeii

LIFE AT THE TOP
The hot, dry regions of the Southwest have preserved
many organic materials, such as plant remains and
coprolites (preserved feces). Pueblo settlements were
constructed on the plains and later on sides of cliffs for
better defense (above). In the 1920s, A. E. Douglass
pioneered the technique of dendrochronology (pp. 54–55)
on wood preserved in these pueblos. This permits wood
used in the various rooms to be precisely dated and helps
reconstruct the building history of the pueblos.

Preserved by ice

THE COLDEST REGIONS ON EARTH, such as Alaska, Siberia, Greenland, and the Alps, can act as a freezers, preserving burials, accident victims, and their possessions, and anything else buried in the frozen ground. The soft tissue of well-preserved bodies gives valuable information about what diseases they died from and what they ate. Analysis shows ancient Inuit often had black lungs from breathing in oil-lamp smoke and they lived mainly on marine foods like fish and seals. High cholesterol levels from their blubber-rich diet caused heart disease. Ice has also preserved wood, food, and garments – parkas, boots, and trousers, and a wonderful array of organic finds from the chiefs' barrows of Pazyryk in Siberia.

Chain stitch embroidery on silk saddlecloth of a pheasant or phoenix

FLOWN FAR FROM HOME
The Pazyryk saddles were made of two joined leather cushions stuffed with deer hair, with wooden bows front and back and a felt cover, usually decorated with cutout felt designs. One cover is a priceless Chinese silk, possibly made made for the marriage of a princess.

Leather ear and horn were detachable

Postures of animals like this curved ram are typical of Pazyryk's artistic style

RAMMED INTO POSITION
At Pazyryk in Siberia, barrows were erected to cover the wooden burial chambers of chiefs and their women c. 400 B.C. Dug in summer when the ground was soft, the underground, log-built chambers froze during their first winter and never thawed again – until they were excavated in the 1940s, using boiling water. Dendrochronology (pp. 54–55) on the logs showed that the five excavated barrows were built over a period of 48 years. These barrows preserved a rich array of artifacts made from various organic materials.

This side of a leather flask from Barrow 1 has a mosaic pattern of white and blue fur shapes

Pieces of leopard skin make up the reverse side

IN THE BAG
The Pazyryk graves yielded many fur and leather containers, like those used by modern nomadic tribes. One flask in Barrow 2 had contained cheese, while others still had plant remains in them, including narcotic hemp seeds and imported coriander. Small clay bottles had once contained *koumiss* (fermented mare's milk). Such details show that the lives of the people of Pazyryk were similar to those of their horse-keeping neighbors, the Scythians, described by Greek and Roman authors.

Horn frontal plate from saddle of one of seven sacrificed horses in Barrow 2

RIDING INTO THE SUNSET
The people of Pazyryk were horse-riding herders, keeping cattle, sheep, goats, and especially horses, which they raised for meat, milk, and skins and traded with the settled peoples of western Asia and China. The chiefs buried here were accompanied by their sacrificed riding horses. The horse trappings included saddles, leather bridles decorated with wooden or horn carvings, and horses' face masks bearing elaborate headdresses.

Gorytus (bow case and quiver)

Horned tiger

Stylized goose

Felt wall hanging shows typical horse and archery equipment

DRESSED TO KILL
The Pazyryk barrows are rich in art. Felt cutout designs portray carnivorous beasts attacking animals. Wooden carvings show men with thick beards. The felt wall hanging from Barrow 5 has riders sporting fine mustaches. The buried chiefs themselves were clean-shaven, but one had an artificial beard made of human hair on a leather strip.

Small carnivore

Deer-shaped monster with elaborate antlers

Tattoos on right arm display predators and their victims, some half mythological

SCARRED FOR LIFE
The burials at Pazyryk did not freeze immediately, so although textiles and wooden objects survived intact, the flesh of sacrificed horses had time to decay, leaving only their skeletons. The human bodies had been embalmed and so were better preserved. The body of a chief from Barrow 2 bore the remains of elaborate tattoos. The tattoos had probably been made by pricking the design deeply into the skin and rubbing soot into it, which gave it a bluish tinge.

Marine archeology

THE SEA HAS YIELDED some extraordinarily well-preserved remains of wrecked ships and drowned settlements, but it is not a gentle preserver. Undersea remains are attacked by salt, marine organisms, and currents. But once the remains settle into the seabed and are covered with silts, their physical destruction virtually ceases. Locating wrecks, like England's *Mary Rose*, is made very difficult by the seabed's shifting silts, but sonar devices can assist reconnaissance. Poor visibility hampers underwater excavation and photography, although the ability to approach remains from any angle allows three-dimensional video recording, impossible on land. Because of buoyancy, physical excavation is easier underwater, but excavators are restricted by the time they can safely work there.

LIFTING THE *MARY ROSE*
Submerged in the seabed for centuries, the *Mary Rose*'s starboard, or right, side survived virtually intact. Excavated between 1966 and 1982, the contents of the hull were carefully recorded and removed. The fragile hull was lifted, using a special tubular steel frame, into a steel cradle lined with air bags. On October 11, 1982, the *Mary Rose* was brought to the surface.

First the hull was lifted onto the cradle underwater, providing support for raising it above water

THE PRIDE OF THE FLEET
The *Mary Rose* (inaccurately but attractively depicted above), was built for England's Henry VIII in 1509–1510. One of the most advanced vessels of her time, she sank during a battle with a French invasion fleet in 1545.

LIFE ON THE *MARY ROSE*
This model shows the surviving portion of the *Mary Rose*'s hull. The galley held a large firebox and four copper caldrons. On the deck above, neatly stacked plates and bowls were found. The injured or sick were laid around the companionway leading out of the hold. Better medical care was provided on the main deck where the barber-surgeon's cabin was located. Bones of many of the *Mary Rose*'s crew and soldiers showed that some died trying to escape. The ship went down so fast that many died where they stood.

Model of the *Mary Rose*'s hull, as she lay on the seabed

Flint ballast in hold kept ship well down in the water

Stored logs used for galley fuel, cables, and barrels of tar

Steel support cradle

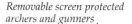

Removable screen protected
archers and gunners

THE *MARY ROSE* RECONSTRUCTED
The recovery of well-preserved wrecks
like the *Mary Rose* provides us with a
wealth of detail about the shipbuilding
methods of their time, information not
available from contemporary illustrations.
The hull of the *Mary Rose* was carvel-built.
Her guns on the main gundeck were fired
through gunports with wooden gunport lids,
while on the weather deck, visible here, wooden
blinds that protected the men against enemy fire
or heavy seas could be removed to run out the guns.

Model of
the *Mary Rose*,
viewed from the
port side (above)

Main
deck
gunport

Swivel gun

Hatch

Upper deck
gunport

Bonaventure
mast

Bowcastle
guns

Mizzen-
mast

Bronze gun in front
of sterncastle

Model of the
Mary Rose
viewed from
above

UNDER THE SEA
Seabed silts can often be
easily excavated with hands
or brushes and the spoil (waste
soil) removed with airlifts. But
these silts are also easily stirred
up by currents or the divers themselves, making the problem of
poor visibility worse.

Castle deck –
the highest deck
in the ship

Barber-surgeon's cabin
contained his chest of
medicines and shaving
equipment

Ointments and field dressings
were among the barber-surgeon's
equipment, as was a wooden mallet
used with an amputation knife

CONSTANT CONSERVATION
The cradle in which the *Mary Rose* was lifted
still supports her in the dry dock where, in
order to preserve the wood, she is sprayed
with chilled water for at least 20 hours
each day. Regular tests ensure
that physical and biological
decay does not occur.

Main deck held guns
as well as carpenter's and
barber-surgeon's cabins
– where many men were
trapped when the ship sank

Orlop deck for stowing
stores, equipment, food,
hand weapons, and
personal possessions

Oak hull is
carvel-built
(smooth, edge-to-
edge planking)

Stern
post

Elm
keel

Galley

Continued on next page

Conserving and treating

Some organic materials like leather and wood can be preserved under the sea, while others like horn and linen are destroyed by marine micro-organisms. Much of the *Mary Rose*'s iron has corroded away, leaving only stains to show what was once there. What survived had to be stabilized to prevent further deterioration. Where appropriate, objects were carefully cleaned with brushes, soluble salts washed out, and insoluble iron corrosion products removed using chemicals.

Turned beechwood bowl inscribed on both sides

WOODEN BOWL

Although wooden objects preserved underwater retain their appearance, the internal structure of the wood is broken down. To preserve them, the water must be replaced with polyethylene glycol (PEG), a type of wax. First, soluble salts are removed by washing and insoluble salts removed by soaking in a chemical solution. The object is soaked in a series of increasingly strong PEG solutions to replace the water in it with PEG. Then it is freeze-dried and stored in a humid environment.

Slashed decoration on high-vamped leather shoe

LEATHER SHOE

Various leather objects were recovered from the *Mary Rose*, including shoes – some still on skeletons' feet. Clothing included woolen stockings, caps, and sleeves. Silk, satin, and lace trimmings survived.

Inscription of Henry VIII

Emblem of the Tudor Rose

Bronze muzzle-loading gun (2500 lb, 1135 kg) was loaded with a solid cast-iron shot when recovered

Reproduction wheeled carriage built of elm with wrought-iron fastenings

CANNON CONSERVATON

Encrustations on the *Mary Rose*'s wrought- and cast-iron cannon were chipped away before the guns were stabilized by heating them in a hydrogen reduction furnace. This turned the oxidized (rusted) iron back into metallic iron. Bronze objects were cleaned of harmful chemicals by repeated washing.

SURE SHOT

All the *Mary Rose*'s guns were found loaded and ready to fire. Various types of ammunition were used by her gunners, including massive stone cannonballs, lead and cast-iron shot. Two-piece molds for casting small lead shot were found at the stern of the ship.

Large stone shot weighs 22 lb (10 kg)

Stone shot weighs 10 lb (4.5 kg)

Iron shot weighs 14 lb (6 kg)

Medium stone shot

Hinged lid

Horn reinforcements on the bows have disintegrated

FRAGILE FLAGON
Pewter must be treated to remove marine encrustations and harmful chemicals, although some objects, like this flagon, are too fragile and must be stabilized as found. Pewter vessels belonged to the *Mary Rose*'s officers, while the soldiers and crew used wooden plates and drinking vessels (tiggs). Also found aboard were meat, vegetables, fruit, herbs, and spices. Wooden and pottery jars in the barber-surgeon's chest contained oint-ments and medicines.

Encrusted pewter caused by action of barnacles and other micro-organisms underwater

Bubbles show that pewter flagon has been conserved, but it can never be restored to its former silvery sheen without risk of object disintegrating

WOODEN BOWS
Despite the importance of the English longbow, no surviving examples had been known to exist until the discoveries from the *Mary Rose*. Some archery equipment was still stored in chests, while other longbows were found with the archers at action stations, ready to defend the ship. Other surviving archery equipment included leather wristguards and 24-hole leather disks in which arrows were stored.

Pewter flagon – over 70 pieces of pewter were recovered from the *Mary Rose*

Yew bows were skillfully cut to provide both strength and flexibility

Sturdy base to avoid movement when ship was sailing

Freshwater preservation

WETLAND SITES such as peat bogs and fens (marshes), are an archeologist's dream. Artifacts from past daily lives have been very well preserved, because the oxygen needed by bacteria which cause organic remains to decay is absent. Wood, leather, and other organic materials from wetland sites give us a much more complete picture than from dry sites, while plant, snail, and insect remains provide valuable information on local environments. However, acid peat bogs destroy materials like pottery and calcium in bones, which survive on dry land sites. But wetland sites do present some problems. During excavation, fragile, waterlogged remains must be kept wet, and excavators must be very careful not to crush them.

Grass roots (living layer of peat)

Pieces of wood denote remains of ancient structures

Plant fiber – such organic material allows the sequence of the peat development to be radiocarbon dated (pp. 54–55)

Head shows he had been hit with blunt instrument, strangled, and his throat cut

Slot in closely fitting wooden box for a sharpening stone, but it was not found

Fingernails show that, like many bog bodies, he had not done rough manual work

WET AND DAMP
Peat slowly forms from vegetation in waterlogged areas, over thousands of years. Commercial exploitation and land drainage are rapidly destroying peat bogs, along with the evidence they contain. Examination of the sides of drainage ditches in England's East Anglian fens led to the discovery of Flag Fen, a remarkable artificial island from the late Bronze Age.

BOGMAN
Peat bogs from Northern Europe have yielded startling finds of well-preserved bodies. Most (probably religious sacrifices) belong to the Iron Age. England's Lindow Man is typical – he had been executed and laid naked in a boggy pool. Scientific investigation can reveal much about bog bodies – Lindow Man's blood group is "O" and charred bread was in his gut.

Leaf shape was typical of late Bronze Age swords

Bronze stopper

Bead

Fibula (like modern safety pin)

Swan's neck pin

Miniature tin wheel

Bronze-plated brooch

Bronze stick pin

TREASURED TOOLS
This pair of bronze shears in a wooden box from Flag Fen was a unique find. Previously, only iron shears had been found. Probably of Iron Age date, they could have been used for shearing sheep and for cutting anything from willow wands to hair. Lindow Man's mustache had been trimmed with shears shortly before his death.

JEWELED ASSORTMENT
These spectacular Iron Age ornaments, all imperfect or deliberately damaged, were among the discoveries from Flag Fen island. Many were locally made, but the unusual wheel was probably from Switzerland. Pins and brooches were used for fastening clothing.

Verdegris – green patina formed on bronze surface after exposure to waterlogged peat over a long period of time

Well-defined midrib

Socket for wooden handle

Swords like this were made in Europe in the Bronze Age, around 1800 B.C.

Spearhead – an uncommon offering at Flag Fen

Break in this sword was done deliberately before it was thrown into the water

Late Bronze Age (c. 1000 B.C.) swords were among the most common offerings at Flag Fen

OFFERINGS TO THE GODS

A 0.6-mi (1-km) line of posts, perhaps a territorial boundary, led from dry land out to the artificial island of Flag Fen. Masses of late Bronze Age and Iron Age objects, particularly swords and pins, as well as animal and some human bones, deposited all along the inshore side of the post alignment. Depositing fine expensive objects in watery places may have been a religious practice in Iron Age Europe.

Distinctive shape is useful for dating by typology

WOODEN BARRIER

Any wooden structure from the prehistoric period is a rare find – and a nightmare to excavate. Much of the work carried out at Flag Fen has been done while uncomfortably suspended above the wooden posts on horizontal scaffolding. The five rows of oak posts formed a 0.6-mi (1-km) long barrier. Its floor was covered with wood chippings and white sand.

Split-oak plank – before invention of saws, timbers were split using wooden wedges

Slot through which plank was pegged to ground

In oak timbers such as these, dendrochronology (pp. 54–55) is used to work out building sequence at Flag Fen

Upright posts stood over 6 ft (2 m) high

TIMBERS FROM FLAG FEN

The principal timbers at Flag Fen were oak and alder with some ash. Some of the oak was used as roundwood, but most had been split into planks. Horizontal timbers were carefully fixed in place by pegs, which were made of coppiced wood, so indicating local woodland management (pp. 46–47). Details in the five rows of posts show the expertise of Bronze Age carpentry.

Distortion in some wood at Flag Fen caused by drying out

Sharpened end for driving timber directly into ground – sometimes marks of ax used for shaping the wood are visible

Conservation of materials

MANY REMAINS OF THE PAST have survived well – until they are discovered and exposed to modern conditions. Often excavated materials must be treated and stabilized to prevent any deterioration (decay). An exception is material to be dated or scientifically analyzed – this must be delivered to the laboratory as found. For example, waterlogged wood must be kept wet, while iron, such as the *Mary Rose*'s cannons, may be heated to stabilize the metal. Objects must be cleaned, either mechanically or chemically. Often this is done on site, although delicate remains are cleaned in the laboratory. Once conserved, objects are ready to be studied or displayed.

Pottery shards, or pieces, emerging from the soil of the Jordanian site of Tell es-Sa'idiyeh (pp. 22–23)

Glue is applied in an extremely thin layer

The matching shards, one edge glued, are carefully aligned so they fit together

A FIRM HAND
Wherever possible, modern conservation is durable but also reversible. The synthetic adhesive used on this jar was selected with these considerations in mind. A very thin layer of adhesive is applied so as not to distort the reassembled pot.

Sand allows joined shards to be supported at the necessary angle

STICKING TOGETHER
The adhesives used in conservation often dry quite slowly so that the conservator, or restorer, has time to get the join right. Masking tape is taped over at right angles to the join, front and back, to support it while the glue is drying. Masking tape is used because its stretchiness keeps the join under tension.

STANDING IN THE SAND
The joined pieces are left to dry in a tray filled with sand. The gradual reassembly of a pot starts with the rim or the base, whichever is more complete. Once the glue is completely dry, the masking tape can be removed.

As the vessel takes shape, the pieces begin to support each other

A CIRCLE OF SHARDS
Although most pottery from excavations is broken and incomplete, sometimes enough pieces survive from one vessel to make a complete reconstruction. First the shards are cleaned by gentle washing in water. If they have absorbed salts from the surrounding soil, they are soaked and resoaked in tap water until all the salts have dissolved out. The shards are now laid out in order – like a jigsaw puzzle.

Base is often the most resilient part of a pot and so survives well

GETTING PLASTERED

Modern repair and restoration must be unobtrusive, but obvious on close examination. Missing bits in pottery are filled in with plaster of Paris. First a sheet of heated wax is molded against a part of the inside of the pot – its shape should match that of the missing piece. When the wax cools and hardens, it is fastened with masking tape behind the hole to support the plaster. As soon as the plaster sets, the conservator smooths it with a fine scalpel.

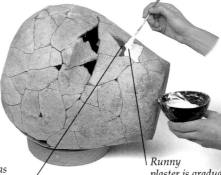

Broken features, such as decorations, spouts, and handles, are clues to matching up adjacent shards

Wax backing acts both as support and as mold for the plaster

Runny plaster is gradually applied into the hole

Rim shards are like the edge pieces of a jigsaw – a good place to start assembling the puzzle

Shards of a pottery jar from an olive-oil factory found at the Jordanian site of Tell es-Sa'idiyeh, c. 2600 B.C., where oil was stored or exported

Spout of vessel

Ring supports jar at any angle during restoration

SPOT THE DIFFERENCE

When the plaster is quite dry, its surface is rubbed down with fine abrasive papers, taking care not to scratch the original pot. It is now ready to be painted, using a color that blends in with the color of the pot itself. The color match should look the same at a distance, but should be distinguishable from the pot at close range.

TOGETHER WE STAND

This now complete "hole-mouth" jar was used in making olive oil. Olives, soaked in hot water and crushed, were placed in this jar to settle. The pulp and water would sink to the bottom, and the pure olive oil would float to the top, to be poured off through the spout.

Continued on next page

Painstaking processes

Conservation begins with stabilization to minimize further deterioration. The necessary conditions must be provided to ensure that objects remain stable. This may involve controlling temperature, humidity, and lighting, and taking precautions against air pollution, mold, and pests. Objects may need to be investigated and cleaned. Some may need to be repaired and restored. The golden rule of modern conservators is that all treatments should be reversible – glues must be soluble, mends or patches must be easy to distinguish from the original object and easy to remove, and treatments must not chemically alter the object. Modern scientific advances have greatly aided conservators, providing a range of useful synthetic materials like adhesives, sophisticated tools and techniques for cleaning and reassembling, and a battery of instruments to examine objects. But it is still a slow and painstaking job, as each object has to be treated individually.

Conserved half of bowl, 1st century A.D.

X ray of corroded bowl

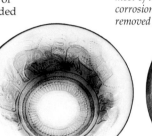

Interior of bowl with most of the surface corrosion removed

A LOOK INSIDE
Machines that can "look into" objects are invaluable to the conservator. X rays are particularly useful, allowing the conservator to assess the condition and nature of an object, such as the pewter flagon from the *Mary Rose* (pp. 34–35). This may be important in determining the treatment it receives.

COMPLICATED CONSERVATION
X rays revealed an elaborate and decorative frieze beneath the corroded exterior of this bowl. The decorated surface was revealed by removing the corrosion, fragment by fragment, with a scalpel under a microscope. The contrast with the bowl's half-cleaned exterior is startling. Chemicals are sometimes used to remove corrosion in order to reveal the original surface of metal objects. They were not used on this bowl because they might have damaged the decorated surface.

Unconserved half of copper alloy bowl from the United Arab Emirates

Parts of the top and sides of the skull were missing

Piece of cranium, or skullcap, c. 2nd century B.C.

Tunic, from 14th century A.D., of plain woven linen, lined with a somewhat coarser woven cotton fabric

Mandible, or lower jaw

FALLING TO PIECES
This broken Iron Age skull from southern England was found wearing a bronze headband. Before reaching the conservation laboratory, the earth was cleaned from the inside of the pieces of bone. Further cleaning was gently undertaken in the laboratory, particularly around the edges to ensure a good join. The crumbling edges were also strengthened. Then the pieces were glued together. Large gaps made much of the skull weak, so they were filled in and painted in a shade close to the color of the skull.

Tooth

Egyptian hieroglyphics from The Book of the Dead

A dark blue striped silk fabric edged the neckline

After turning right side out, the backing was adjusted so that its weave ran parallel to that of the tunic

Curved suture needle makes the task of stitching on a flat surface easier

FRAGILE TEXTILE
This damaged and very brittle linen tunic came to the conservation laboratory inside out. Its fragility meant that it first had to be mounted on a supportive backing made of new cotton cloth, dyed to a color close to that of the tunic. The backing was sewn to the tunic, with extra stitching around the worst holes, and the tunic was carefully turned right side out. The temporary stitching was removed and the damaged areas repaired with almost invisible stitches using matching silk thread.

THE BOOK OF THE DEAD
Before conservation, this piece of shroud was a crumpled mass. Water vapor was used to relax the linen, gently separating the fragments. Then the shroud was opened out carefully. The text enabled the pieces to be related correctly, then mounted on paper.

Heron

Linen shroud
(c. 1450 B.C.)
after conservation

Human remains

THE REMAINS OF HUMAN BODIES give direct evidence of our past. Bones give some information, soft tissue more, and scientific aids, like CAT scans (horizontal 2-D X rays of the body) and microchemical analyses, reveal amazing details. We can find out what people ate, the work they did, how long they lived, and what illnesses they suffered. Different inherited bone structures provide clues to relationships between individuals. Ancient DNA, or genetic material, yield important data on human evolution. Even footprints give clues, showing that Lucy and her relatives (pp. 6–7) walked upright.

Skin molded over model of Ice Man's skull

Pegs mark key points on the skull where thickness of soft tissues is known

Nose cartilage has been added – its shape depends partly on the skull's shape

IN THE FLESH
Soft tissue, preserved in such individuals as the Ice Man, who died in the Alps more than 4,000 years ago, is very informative. Stomach contents show what the person's last meal contained. Hair styles and body decoration can survive, as can parasites and traces of viruses. Whole bodies reveal far more than just bones do about ancient diseases.

GET STUFFED
Ancient Egyptians mummified (artificially preserved) their important dead. The corpse's internal organs were removed and the remaining body preserved by packing crystals of natron (a kind of soda) around it. The body was stuffed with leaves or sawdust to restore the natural contours of the body. Finally, the mummified body was carefully bandaged in linen.

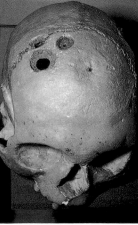

A DRASTIC CURE!
The bizarre practice of trepanning (cutting a disk of bone from a living person's skull) was perhaps used to treat headaches or relieve pressure on brain tumors – many patients survived! Other skeletons show deliberate mutilation to fit society's idea of beauty, such as binding a baby's head to change its shape. Skeletons may also reveal accidental injury or abnormal wear on bones caused by certain kinds of jobs.

FACE TO FACE
We are able to reconstruct what people of the past looked like by using clues from bone structure and our knowledge of anatomy. Another interesting method was used in the reconstruction of the skull from a richly furnished tomb at Vergina in Greece. Comparison of the reconstructed head with literary sources and portraits identified him as Philip of Macedon, Alexander the Great's father.

Hair was well preserved by cold, arid conditions

This head is from one of the Arica mummies – mummification was the result of an earthquake

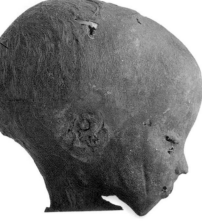

Age clues such as tooth eruption indicate this child was about two years old

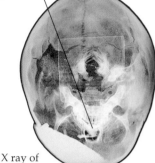

X ray of Peruvian child's skull

PERUVIAN PEOPLE
A study of skeletons buried at Arica in Peru, c. 5800–2000 B.C., shows that it was rare for individuals to live more than 50 years. On average, women died before men. Many women had deformed ankle joints, suggesting that they had worked in a crouched position. Such work-related stress on a skeleton can often be detected. Archers from the *Mary Rose* (pp. 32–35), for example, revealed spinal injuries and thickened forearms.

THE INSIDE STORY
Human teeth emerge and bones stop growing at known ages in childhood, so "aging" children's remains is possible. Adults are harder to age, but wear on teeth and structural changes in their skeletons can give some clues. Now, new scientific analyses may give a better indication of age.

Stain of bones in the sand body lights up under ultraviolet light and can be photographed to reveal the skeleton

A GHOST IN THE SAND
It is an amazing fact of modern science that we can study bodies that have disappeared. At Sutton Hoo (pp. 26–27), acid sandy soil completely destroyed the remains of buried Anglo-Saxons – but the bodies (above) left telltale stains in the soil. Some biochemical elements, like amino acid from proteins, survive decay. Even in sand bodies, these can be detected, revealing the individual's sex and blood group.

Eye color must be guessed

AN EYE TO THE FUTURE
The Ice Man was accidentally preserved where he died, but most human remains come from burials. Neanderthal skeletons with carefully placed offerings were the first deliberate burials. Neanderthals also cared for their disabled – an individual from Shanidar in Iraq was too crippled to fend for himself, but survived to old age. Some cultures cremate the dead – surprisingly, even cremated remains are very informative. Other cultures expose their dead. Evidence of this in Neolithic Britain comes from the cemetery at Hambledon Hill, where many incomplete skeletons were found, including the lower part of a body gnawed by dogs.

Skin condition and color of hair must be guessed, as the skull gives no clues to what these looked like

Food and environment

WHAT DID PEOPLE IN THE PAST EAT? How did they get their food? Obviously, we will never know all the answers to these questions, because most food is eaten and many food remains perish. But archeologists find clues in their knowledge of what foods were available at the time, which tools might have been used to prepare them, and how modern groups find food. Plant foods do not usually survive, while bones do – this gives us an unbalanced picture of past diet. Although our evidence is incomplete, we can begin to see how people found ways to increase their food supply, using tools and controlling plants and animals. But people are still animals, subject to the laws of nature. Remembering this helps us to understand how our ancestors got their food.

The aurochs (*Bos primigenius*), ancestor of our domestic cattle, was a vast and savage beast

Three fish hooks from ancient Egypt

SKEWERED SKULL
For most of human existence, people have lived by hunting and gathering wild foods. Plants must have played a major role in the diet of people living in most tropical and temperate areas. Only in harsh arctic environments would meat have constituted the main source of food. But since plant remains do not preserve well, most archeological evidence is of hunting.

Harpoon was fastened to wooden shaft

GETTING HOOKED
Evidence of past diet from food remains can be supplemented by interpreting the functions of particular artifacts. Further clues come from the kind of wear or residues (such as "silica gloss" on tools used for harvesting plants). These hooks give evidence of fishing, but the harpoons could have been used to hunt a variety of creatures.

OLD FISH BONES
Generally fish bones are small and fragile, so they, like plant remains, are often under-represented among archeological finds. Identifying fish bones tells us what species were being eaten, and some provide evidence of the time of year when they were caught. Deep-sea species indicate that people had developed boats for off shore navigation.

Central prong was attached to a rope

Fish bones from Tell es-Sa'idiyeh in Jordan

Three Egyptian harpoons – fish and hippopotamuses were hunted with such weapons

Hook formed by mammoth's tail held spear before it was thrown

Tusk

A USEFUL SPEAR-THROWER
Unlike most other animals, people can extend their natural capabilities by devising and using tools. This beautiful carving of a mammoth (c. 12,000 B.C.), made from a reindeer antler, is also a useful tool.

ABORIGINE HUNTER
An Australian Aborigine is shown using a spear-thrower. By extending the length of his arm, the hunter's spear-thrower allows the spear to be propelled with greater force over a longer distance. By observing such tools in use, archeologists have been able to identify and interpret artifacts from the past, such as the Paleolithic spear-thrower (far left).

44

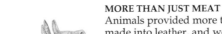

Carts, sleds, or plows could carry loads or people and be pulled by horses, bullocks, llamas, even dogs

MORE THAN JUST MEAT

Animals provided more than just meat. Hides were made into leather, and wool or hair into textiles. Cows, ewes, goats, and even horses gave milk for drinking and for making cheese, butter, and yogurt. The proportions of male and female, and young and old animals on archeological sites indicate the purposes for which they were kept.

Neolithic axe killed this aurochs about 4,000 years ago

MOUNDS OF MOLLUSKS

Shell middens are piles of discarded mollusk (clam, oyster, or mussel) shells, but include other food remains. Although there were a lot of shells, their food value was small. One red deer has more calories than 50,000 oysters! Mollusks were useful for lean periods in seasonally varied diets.

Eye socket

SHEPHERDING

In many parts of the world, the last 10,000 years have seen a shift from hunting animals to herding them. Domestication and the spread of farming communities took many animals far from their original homes – Indian jungle fowl to Europe, for example, and western Asiatic goats to India.

Soay sheep is a primitive breed – more similar to goats than their modern descendants

Nasal cavity

Butchery mark

BUTCHERED BONES

Excavated bones may be fragmentary, but the species of animal they came from can often be identified. Details of shape may allow the age and sex of the animals to be determined, resulting in a picture of the way they were used – for meat, milk, wool, traction (pulling), or transport.

Continued on next page

Carbonized wheat, barley, fig seeds, and grape seeds

Environmental findings

Local weather and environment have always played an important part in quality of life. Archeologists are interested in reconstructing the climate, vegetation, and other environmental aspects of the past – their interests range from personal hygiene to global climatic change. Some aspects of climate and environment have left marks on the landscape such as great valleys carved by glaciers, or ancient beaches left high and dry by changes in sea level. Past climates and environments can also be re-created using micro-organisms from sediments deep in the sea. Soils reflect the conditions in which they were formed. Many small creatures live only in certain environments, and combined with evidence from plant remains, these clues can help reconstruct vegetation, rainfall, temperature, soils, human influences, and other aspects of environments (both local and global).

GROW MORE FOOD
Human population has grown through the ages because we have found ways to control and increase our food supply, including agriculture. Grains, husks, and other plant fragments, such as the remains, above, from a site in Jordan, show that many early farmers grew cereals – wheat, barley, corn, millet, or rice. Probably root crops were equally important in many areas, but they leave no archeological traces.

TOO TEMPTING
Other plant foods were important to early farmers. Central America lacked animals that were suitable for domestication, so beans were a vital source of protein. Initially, farmers used local plants, but gradually, cultivated plants were introduced from other areas. Often agriculture became increasingly intensive, with higher crop yields but more work involved. Population growth may have encouraged this. Greater food supplies also supported trade and industry.

Pomegranates were popular in ancient Egypt

This species of land snail lived on chalky soil

CRAWLING WITH INFORMATION
Microscopic animals from water-logged deposits at York in northern England show both aspects of personal hygiene and daily life. One Roman sewer contained flies from toilets, and a beetle that lived in stored grain, showing that the sewer had drained a granary. Waste from tanning leather was found in York's Viking settlement, including dung beetles (above). Parasite eggs found in cesspits (pp. 6–7) show that worms had infested people's intestines.

FUSSY SNAILS
Vegetation, soils, and climate can be reconstructed from various plant and animal remains. Land snails prefer very specific habitats, so they are excellent indicators of local environment. Changes through time are reflected by changes in the snail population. Beetles, insects, and tiny mammals also give pictures of conditions on land, while aquatic diatoms (single-celled algae) reflect conditions in lakes and pools.

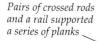
Pairs of crossed rods and a rail supported a series of planks

THE HAND OF MAN

Ancient charcoal shows hunter-gatherers cleared forests with fire. The open land attracted animals to hunt, and encouraged edible plants to grow. Pollen shows changes in vegetation when agriculture was introduced to an area, with trees giving way to cultivated plants and their weeds. The Sweet Track in the Somerset Levels of south-western England was built from trackways of hurdles woven from hazel rods about 5,000 years ago. This shows that hazel was being coppiced (periodically cut down to encourage growth). Woodland management was well developed by these farmers. The Sweet Track also yielded beetles, indicating that when it was built the winters were colder and the summers hotter than nowadays.

UNSAVORY INTEREST

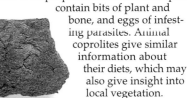

Human coprolites (preserved feces) show what people ate. Dissected examples contain bits of plant and bone, and eggs of infest-ing parasites. Animal coprolites give similar information about their diets, which may also give insight into local vegetation.

Dog coprolites – some are found in water-logged cesspits, others in dry areas

LOST OPPORTUNITIES

Many areas were once inhabited but are no longer. Sometimes the changes are due to human activity – overexploitation, deforestation, or salination caused by irrigation. Elsewhere there may be natural causes as when rivers changed course and farmers followed them. Rock paintings in the Sahara depict domestic cattle that required a much moister habitat. Environmental evidence shows this region once supported woodland, grassland, and lakes, but dried up from 6000 B.C. onward.

Flowering plants produce microscopic pollen grains dispersed by wind or insects

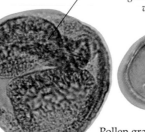

Pollen grains of a pine tree

Pollen grains of plantain (a type of weed)

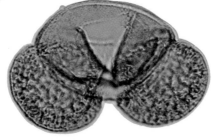

MICROSCOPIC BEAUTY

Pollen grains give clues for environmental and climatic reconstruction at all levels. In domestic situations, pollen indicates plant foods being eaten at that time. Pollen samples from soil reflect local ecology, while pollen samples from lakes or bogs give a picture of vegetation over a wider region. Changes through time in trees and plants can indicate shifts in vegetation because of human activities or climatic change. The widely fluctuating global climate in the last two and half million years has been reconstructed from both deep-sea deposits and long pollen records, and their results broadly agree.

Investigating daily life

ARCHEOLOGY PLAYS A MAJOR ROLE in understanding the past. What do artifacts such as these finds from Roman Britain tell us? Some information is straightforward. Analyses of artifacts tell much about ancient technology. Often what the artifacts were used for can be determined by microscopic investigations revealing food residues or patterns of wear. Discovering certain objects together or in a particular context can also help in understanding their use. Archeologists wish to find out about other aspects of the past, such as social organization, but evidence for these is harder to interpret.

FASHIONABLE FOOTWEAR
Fashion has always influenced the clothes people wear, but rarely are archeologists able to recover ancient clothing They have to be content with artistic representations and small surviving fittings such as belt or shoe buckles, or the jewelry used to fasten cloaks or tunics.

Leather clothing preserved in a waterlogged site

Roman-style sandal cut from a single piece of leather

Manacles from the 1st-2nd century A.D. show that slave trading continued under Roman rule

ON A PLATE
Romans used metal as well as pottery for tableware, such as this plate. People ate with fingers, the point of a knife, or a spoon (such as this 1st-2nd-century A.D. pewter example). Forks were a much later invention. Food remains add to the knowledge of Roman eating habits that we have from such literary sources as the famous cookbook by Apicius. Oyster shells are a very common find from Roman Britain.

Oysters were a cheap food in England until the 1800s when they were destroyed by disease

ENSLAVED
Roman literary sources mention Britain as an important source of slaves, even before the conquest in A.D. 43. Finds of iron slave manacles and chains with neck rings vividly confirm the existence of this British export. Not all slaves endured harsh conditions. Many were valued members of the family circle and were eventually freed or bought their freedom with their savings.

The value of typology

Typological classification is important in archeologists' work. Taking a group of pots, an archeologist asks, "How can I sort these to find out more about them and the society they belonged to?" Differences in pots' clays, shapes, decoration, and manufacturing techniques can be examined. Style changes are useful for dating, pots from different places indicate trade, and variations in quality can show social status.

Clay used to manufacture this mortarium had pieces of grit added to produce the desired rough surface

MIXING IT
A *mortarium* (or mixing bowl) was a common feature of the Romano-British kitchen. Its gritty surface was useful for grinding ingredients into powder. Its large size could hold a great many ingredients for mixing together, and its pouring lip helped remove the completed mixture – sausages, perhaps.

TOP QUALITY
Technically perfect, samian was Roman Britain's top luxury tableware. Manufactured mainly in Gaul (France), samian was made in elaborate molds. Often the maker's name was stamped on the base. By studying the pattern of finds carrying these names, we get a clear picture of the industrial of samian and its wide distribution.

Name of maker (Igocatus) is stamped on the base of this samian bowl found in London, England

Amphorae *were stacked horizontally in transit – when in use they were propped against a wall*

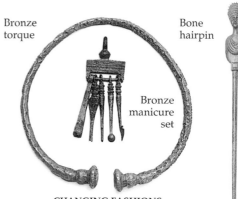

Bronze torque

Bronze manicure set

Bone hairpin

POTS OF PLENTY
Some pottery traveled around the ancient world as disposable or reusable containers, similar to our glass or plastic bottles. They provide evidence for trade goods they were designed to carry. *Amphorae* (tall tapering pottery jars) were used in the Roman world to transport not only dry goods, but also wine, olive oil, and *garum* – a sauce made from fermented fish frequently used to season cooking.

CHANGING FASHIONS
Long bone hairpins were used in elaborate Roman hairdos of the 1st century A.D. (above). Later, shorter pins showed hairstyles had become simpler. A bronze manicure set was worn on a Roman lady's belt – its quality and decoration show it was a prized personal ornament.

A ROMAN KITCHEN
This Roman kitchen was reconstructed using both historical and archeological evidence. Humbler items, such as a *mortarium*, coarse vessels and *amphorae*, glass storage jars, and some kitchen utensils, were frequent finds at Roman settlement sites. Evidence of bones and plant residues from excavations, combined with documenting and pictures, give us a good idea of what Romans ate.

COOKING POT
Most Roman pottery was mass-produced, and some traveled considerable distances from manufacturer to user. Coarse cooking pots of many different types were usually made locally. This grayware was made in southeast England and used in Roman London.

Pot would have been set in embers to cook food

Carrot-shaped *amphora* stored dry foods – an analysis of residues from one *amphora* showed traces of wheat flour

Tapering form of the amphora *makes it easy to lift and balance on a shoulder, but its handles were weak*

Nene Valley potteries first began to supply the demands of the locally-based military shortly after the conquest of Britain in A.D. 43

Hunting scenes often decorated Nene Valley "hunt cups"

NENE VALLEY WARE
England's Nene Valley, with good clays, plenty of timber, and a well-developed road and water transport network, became one of the main pottery manufacturing areas in Roman Britain. One of the main products of these potteries was Nene Valley ware, a fine tableware decorated with semi-liquid clay applied like cake icing – a cheaper alternative to samian.

Clues to trade and industry

SCIENCE PROVIDES MANY TOOLS for understanding how trade and industry were carried out in the past. For example, chemical and physical analyses of metal spears can show us which ores they were made from, where these ores came from, and their makers' skills and technological knowledge. Even the source of the stone used to make a prehistoric ax, or of the clay from a Roman pot, can be identified by scientific analysis. Matching artifacts to their source in this way is a complex process, but it is a rewarding one, for it tells archeologists much about how societies traded with each other to obtain the raw materials they needed or the luxuries they wanted. The pattern of these trade links also provides information about how the societies involved related to each other, and how they were organized.

Mace wrapped around nutmeg

Nutmeg

ALONG THE SPICE ROUTE
Nowadays, food can be preserved for long periods by freezing. Other methods, such as salting or drying, were necessary until recently so food was often uninteresting or bad tasting. Spices could disguise this and so were highly prized. Since many were acquired from distant lands, they were expensive and often traded for gold.

Simple, one-piece mold for making early cast objects

BEAUTIFUL LAPIS
Ancient societies of Egypt, western Asia, and India knew only one source of lapis lazuli – at Badakshan in Afghanistan. Archeology shows that lapis was first exchanged locally among neighboring groups, but finally came under the political control of the Indus peoples.

Flat ax – later axes had raised edges to attach them to handles

Socket for a handle

Chisel

Tiny blade of obsidian (natural volcanic glass)

Flint tools (center, right)

FITTING THE MOLD
Copper was first used as an attractive "stone" with the unusual property of changing shape when hammered. People then began to heat and smelt copper and alloy (combine) it with other minerals, such as arsenic, antimony, tin, and lead, to improve aspects of its performance. Early objects in copper or bronze often imitated the shape of familiar stone objects. Bronze tools and weapons eventually largely replaced stone ones, but they were initially more important as status symbols.

GRIMES GRAVES
Flint mining and stone quarrying began early in the Neolithic period as demand grew for axes to clear forests for agriculture. Often small-scale, there were also some much larger examples, such as Grimes Graves mines in eastern England.

NATURAL GLASS
Obsidian was prized by past societies in western Asia, Europe, and Central America. Using scientific analysis to match obsidian artifacts with limited sources of the glass shows how it was traded among prehistoric groups.

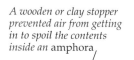
A wooden or clay stopper prevented air from getting in to spoil the contents inside an amphora

Large handle for lifting heavy amphora

THE SILK ROAD

The Chinese controlled the lively trade route to the west through the inhospitable central Asian desert. Buddhism was carried along this route from India to China. Three cultures come together in this painting – a 9th-century Chinese silk scroll showing an Indian Bodhisattva (a future Buddha) holding a Persian glass vase.

Painting was found by Sir Aurel Stein at Tun-huang in China

Sassanian glass bowl (c. 500 A.D.)

Pottery vessel, a typical Nubian type exported to Egypt, 16th-century B.C.

ANOTHER *AMPHORA*

Surviving wrecks of Roman ships carrying *amphorae* give a good picture of the way in which trade was conducted in Roman times. *Amphorae* often bore the name of their manufacturer. Often other stamps indicated their contents, which can today be verified by chemical analysis of the residues inside the containers.

UP THE NILE

Egypt had extensive commercial and political relations with Nubia, its neighbor up the Nile. Many of the products from sub-Saharan Africa reached Egypt through Nubia – skins, elephant ivory, ebony, ostrich feathers, and exotic beasts such as baboons and giraffes. Many aspects of life in Nubia were strongly influenced by Egyptian culture.

EGYPTIAN TRADE

Wall paintings, texts, and archeological finds show how extensive Egypt's trade relations were. Here 15th century B.C. envoys from Syria bring goods to Egypt. Objects came from as far away as Minoan Crete; cedarwood for ship-building was a major import from Lebanon. Punt, a mysterious land on the Red Sea, supplied incense. Turquoise and copper were mined in the Sinai Desert.

Buildings of the past

MANY BUILDINGS OF THE PAST have disappeared, but others still stand thousands of years later. Many factors govern survival – the building material (perishable wood or durable stone), the structure's function (permanent religious building or overnight shelter), and activities in the area (undisturbed desert tombs or houses in an ever-changing city). Various factors also determine whether we can trace vanished structures. Postholes will show the foundations of timber buildings, but wooden structures built directly on the ground may be gone forever unless the position of finds inside and out reveals where walls once stood. Excavations recover objects but destroy structures – postholes are dug out and walls removed to expose the layers underneath. All structural information must be recorded carefully in notes, plans, photographs, and sections, since these records are all that will remain.

ANCIENT PEOPLE AT HOME
Our early ancestors' structures are rarely preserved, so the chances of finding them are remote. The discovery, at Terra Amata in France, of a hut 300,000 years old, was incredible luck. Stake holes show that it was built of brushwood, with stones around the outside and stronger posts holding up the roof. The hut collapsed after it was abandoned, but was rebuilt when people returned in the spring.

Victorian building, partially demolished

A WINDOW INTO THE PAST
Successful towns are occupied for centuries, each generation building over the remains of the previous ones. Their early stages are hard to investigate because the modern town gets in the way. When structures are demolished for redevelopment, archeologists can examine small pieces of the town underneath, from which they construct a patchwork picture of the past. This model shows one such excavated "window" into old London.

Deposits that have accumulated since medieval times

Fence enclosing building site in 1881–1882 when this area of London's Gracechurch Street was cleared to build Leadenhall Market

Walls of medieval Leadenhall – in medieval times, London was a major industrial center and international port

Remains of Roman basilica, incorporated into medieval Leadenhall

ETERNAL DEATH
Houses may last a lifetime, but monumental tombs are for eternity. These Egyptian pyramids at Giza, built to house dead pharaohs through a perpetual afterlife, have endured nearly 5000 years. They are a monument now to their laborers, who dragged and levered the massive blocks into place.

PEOPLE UNDERFOOT
Excavated buildings often seem to be made of plain brick or bare stone. But originally they were not so stark. Many houses had painted plaster walls, such as those that survive in Roman Pompeii, along with exquisite floor mosaics, here showing actors preparing for a play.

FULLY FURNISHED
Skara Brae on Orkney, Scotland, gives a rare glimpse inside a Neolithic furnished house, c. 3000 B.C. Timber was scarce on the island, so Skara Brae's builders constructed all the usual furnishings in stone. A freak sandstorm engulfed the settlement, preserving the houses undisturbed, complete with stone shelves, beds, fireplaces – even water tanks for keeping shellfish fresh.

COMPUTER WIZARDRY
The remains of Cluny, the great 11th-century French abbey, were meticulously excavated between 1928 and 1950. In 1990–1991, engineering students working at IBM successfully reconstructed Cluny with a computer, using the excavation records and special software designed for architects. Computer-generated imagery can accurately recreate vanished buildings, but only if the data is sufficient. Evidence for prehistoric structures is often limited to ground plans, but computers can test different reconstructions – an alternative to actually building them (pp. 58–59)!

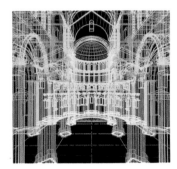

Reconstructing Cluny by computer beginning (bottom) and end (top)

Public buildings, such as this Roman basilica, are often created in enduring materials, such as brick or stone, which survive better than flimsy domestic architecture

Roman arch

Ground surface in 1881–1882

Dating the past

ARCHEOLOGICAL SITES AND OBJECTS are mainly dated by combining stratigraphy (giving a sequence) and typology (identifying artifacts typical of different periods in the sequence). Except in areas with historical records, archeologists had only this loose relative chronology until 1949, when the invention of radiocarbon dating made it possible to date organic remains and the deposits they came from. Many more dating techniques have since appeared. Most are radiometric, based on the rate of decay, or change, of particular radioactive elements. We know how much radioactivity was in an object originally; the object is dated by measuring how much of that radioactive content has decayed. Dating our early ancestors, like *Homo habilis*, well beyond radiocarbon's range, combines several techniques such as K/Ar, fission track dating, reversals in the Earth's magnetic polarity, and biostratigraphy.

Tree rings grow annually – in sensitive trees like oak, rings vary in thickness from year to year, depending on growing conditions

TREE-RING DATING
Fluctuations in the level of C-14 in the atmosphere cause radiocarbon dates, particularly before 1000 B.C., to work out to be more recent than they really should be. Dendrochronology (tree-ring dating) has helped solve this problem. Using many trees, scientists have built up tree-ring sequences going back beyond 7500 B.C. By comparing radiocarbon dates on wood with its true age, known from dendrochronology, scientists have produced a chart converting radiocarbon dates to actual calendar dates.

A REVOLUTION!
A tiny fraction of the carbon in the atmosphere is radioactive. When living things die, this radiocarbon, or C-14, decays at a known rate. By measuring how much radiocarbon remains in organic material, such as bone, shell, or wood and other plant material, scientists can calculate how long ago death occurred.

SCINTILLATING
To radiocarbon-date a bone, a sample is crushed and added to acid to extract the protein (above). This is chemically cleaned and converted to benzene – a liquid used for accurate measuring. The amount of C-14 present when the creature died is then calculated, using the two forms of carbon that don't decay (C-12 and C-13). The amount of C-14 originally present is compared with the amount still remaining. The proportion that has decayed allows a date to be worked out. An alternative method of measuring uses an acceleration mass spectrometer. This measures the amounts of different forms of carbon present in small samples of material, and can date back to 100,000 B.C.

Benzene from the conversion process is dated by liquid scintillation counting

Material being converted to benzene for dating was once living tissue

Section of a vacuum line – used to convert samples to benzene

HOW OLD IS EARLY MAN?

The remains of man's early ancestors lie far beyond the date range of radiocarbon. Radiometric methods such as fission-track dating and potassium-argon dating (K/Ar), which date igneous rocks, provide an indirect date for archeological material in the layers between the rocks. Biostratigraphy is more direct – dated forms in the evolution of such animals as pigs indicate the approximate age of associated archeological material.

Skull of our earliest ancestor *Homo habilis*

ELECTRONS ON THE MOVE

Tiny quantities of radioactive matter occur in the clay used for making pottery. Radioactive decay causes electrons in the pottery structure to be dislodged. These are caught in the crystal lattice of the pot's fabric, where they remain until heated above 932°F (500°C). This took place when the pot was fired, "resetting" the radiometric "clock" to zero. Measuring the extent to which the process of electron displacement has reoccurred allows the date of the pot's firing to be calculated.

Photomultiplier tube

The decorative figures on this terra-cotta were made using a genuine Zapotec mold, but the figure looked wrong and forgery was suspected

SEEING THE LIGHT

A small sample is drilled from pottery to be dated by thermoluminescence (TL). This is crushed and sieved to extract quartz crystals, which are placed on a heater plate (above) and put into a photomultiplier machine. When the electrons pop back into place, they give off an amount of light that is proportional to the age of the pottery and to the amount of radioactive material present.

Drill hole in terra-cotta statue from which a tiny sample has been taken for TL dating

IS IT ORIGINAL?

Pottery is the most common material found in archeological sites of the last 10,000 years. So thermoluminescence (TL), the recently developed technique for dating pottery, is a godsend for archeologists and is invaluable for detecting forgeries (pp. 56–57). For example, the abundance of Zapotec terra-cottas has aroused suspicion. Using TL to date when these figures were made has revealed that many known examples, including this seated god, are recent fakes.

1981.4.16.1

Fakes and forgeries

THE PURPOSE OF FAKING (fraudulently modifying) and forgery (making falsely) is to deceive. Usually this is done for money: making imitations of valuable, but scarce, antiquities and selling them as genuine. Forged documents, from medieval monastic charters to wills and passports, are used to support claims to land, property, identity, or power. Sometimes eccentric individuals make forgeries for the satisfaction of fooling the experts. Some forgeries are crude copies, while others are sophisticated replicas using ancient technology. The skills developed for conservation can be fraudulently misused to restore damaged objects or put together unrelated broken objects (pastiche), to sell as genuine undamaged antiquities.

IN THE UNDERWORLD
Small figures (shabtis) were placed in Egyptian tombs as substitutes for the deceased in the Underworld. Now many forgeries cast in molds have supplemented genuine ones and are easily detected by stylistic inaccuracies and nonsensical inscriptions.

COPYCAT!
Differences between ancient and more recent technology can be used to distinguish forgeries from genuine antiquities. Research into ancient methods has enabled skilled forgers to produce technically convincing objects (far right). These can still be identified as forgeries, however, through the use of scientific techniques like thermoluminescence.

AUTHENTIC OR NOT?
This soapstone figure is said to be from Great Zimbabwe in Africa, where there are similar but larger soapstone columns. It is uncertain whether this figure is genuine; it is suspiciously unworn and has no details of when and where it was found. Such information is vital to show the authenticity of doubtful objects.

Red background produced by firing in air

During firing, the air supply was reduced and the vessel turned black. When air was reintroduced, painted areas stayed black and the rest turned red

Genuine Athenian black-figure-ware vase, 6th century B.C.

Fake teabowl

Brown/black "hare's fur" glaze

Modern forgery using same methods of production as similar vase (left)

MODERN FORGERY
***VS.* ANCIENT ARTIFACT**
The differences between the colorings and glazes on these two teabowls from China is apparent even to the naked eye. The genuine article (right), in dark brown stoneware, has a much more subtle coloring with delicate "hare's fur" markings on its black glaze. The modern forgery (above) has a shiny glaze with similar but cruder markings. The base of the forgery has a well-defined shape, while that of the real artifact is roughly joined to the bowl.

Delicate markings on black glaze

Jian ware teabowl from the Song Dynasty (A.D. 960–1279)

Color of clay is distinctive on this genuine terracotta

Genuine terra-cotta figure of a woman

Drapery is clumsy imitation of genuine terra-cotta

Fake terra-cotta figure of a woman

SPANISH BULL
Assessing the authenticity of ancient works depends on what society knows and expects at the time of their discovery. Archeologists in the 1800s viewed Paleolithic people as uncultured savages, so they were scornful of Marcelino de Sautuola's claim in 1879 to have discovered magnificent Paleolithic paintings at a cave in Altamira in northeastern Spain. They even suggested that the art was forged with his knowledge. De Sautuola's inspired claim for their antiquity was vindicated only after his death with further discoveries of cave art.

TANAGRAS
Despite extensive 19th-century plundering of ancient tombs, demand for fine pieces of classical sculpture was so great that forgeries abounded. Tanagras (draped female figures) were particularly popular. Their diversity has made it difficult to assess their authenticity on stylistic grounds, as many fakes were skillfully put together from unrelated ancient fragments and sold as "restorations."

16th-century forgery of a sestertius (Roman coin) of Claudius

Contemporary counterfeit sestertius, c. A.D. 50

COUNTERFEIT
Despite severe penalties, counterfeiting of official coinage is widespread. Counterfeiters often faked high-value coinage by coating a base-metal core in silver or gold. These ancient fakes are detected by careful analysis of their chemical composition. Generally official coins are die-struck, but forgeries are made using a new die, details differing slightly from the original. An identical copy can be produced by making a mold from a genuine coin in which copies are cast. The resulting detail is less sharp than the original.

Genuine sestertius, c. A.D. 42 , of Claudius, Roman emperor from A.D. 41–54

Experimental archeology

Daub – made from mud, clay, cow dung, hay, and water

WHEN ARCHEOLOGISTS INTERPRET their discoveries, they are often trying to make intelligent guesses from what they already know, from their own experiences and imaginations. Two helpful ways to test their guesses and discover new possibilities are by experimenting (trying out different possibilities) and by ethnographic analogy (looking at how other cultures do things). These approaches not only show that some interpretations do not work while others do, but they may also pinpoint what archeologists might usefully look for in the future.

A GLASTONBURY HOUSE
This unfinished roundhouse shows coppiced hazel rods (wattle) woven between uprights set in postholes and then plastered with daub. The roof had to be pitched at an angle between 45° and 50° to ensure that rainwater would run off, rather than soak the thatch.

Ash flail for separating grain from husks

Flail used for threshing; experiments showed some early breeds of wheat were difficult to thresh

Tongue for harnessing horse or ox behind vallus to push it through crop

Box contained wooden spears, which broke the stalks and collected the grain

Vallus (Roman reaping machine)

Rafters bound to ring tie-beam to support thatch

TOOLS OF THE TRADE
Actual archeological evidence of Iron Age farming is limited, although Roman records show that Iron Age Britain was prosperous, exporting grain and hides. Work at the experimental Butser Iron Age Farm in England has helped fill some of the gaps in our knowledge, demonstrating the efficiency of Iron Age implements. The ard was shown to be suitable for working not only light soils but, contrary to expectation, heavy clay soils as well.

Iron rim applied when red-hot to tighten up the wheel (made of elm, oak, or ash) as iron contracted

Beam of ard went between the pair of oxen and was attached to the yoke

Ard, made of ash, was an early type of plow drawn by a pair of oxen

Handle held by plowman to keep the share correctly angled in the ground

Share ripped through the ground but did not turn it, like a true plow would have

LIFE IN THE ROUND
Much of the work at Butser has focused on reconstructing an Iron Age roundhouse. Archeologists know it was made from a large, central posthole surrounded by a ring of smaller postholes. What structure using this setup would be stable and durable? How was the roof made? This experimental reconstruction helped answer such questions. This large roundhouse is built of ash or oak uprights, interspersed by hazel wattling, plastered with daub, and roofed with thatch on a framework of wooden rafters interwoven with hazel rods, like a spider's web.

ETHNOARCHEOLOGY

Ethnographic evidence is very valuable because it not only shows archeologists the many ways different people make artifacts and provide shelter, clothing, and food, but also gives some insight into other aspects of their lives. However, modern ethnography cannot tell us exactly how the past worked – no two cultures are the same and modern cultures are not "living fossils" of our ancestors' ways of life. Much can be learned about stone tool technology from Australia's Aborigines, who make arrowheads from many modern materials.

Ears of einkorn, one of the earliest wheats cultivated

Old English game fowl were bred from Indian jungle fowl

Grains of einkorn

PRIMITIVE BREEDS

Butser has a range of primitive breeds – cattle, five kinds of sheep, and these Old English game fowl – as similar as possible to ones kept in the Iron Age. Work with these animals highlights aspects of their behavior that would have affected Iron Age farmers – such as the difficulty of confining Soay sheep, given their ability to jump fences. Plowing experiments using small, strong Dexter cattle show their ability to plow much larger areas in a day than previously had been expected.

Cap kept in smoke, but kept out rain, birds, and insects

Lancehead made from beer-bottle glass

Arrowhead made from insulator on telephone pole

Arrowhead made from colored glass

CULTIVATING THE PAST

Experimental cultivation of different cereal grains grown in the Iron Age gives interesting information on yields, disease resistance, weed and weather tolerances, and nutritional content. At Butser, important experiments have also been done on grain storage, showing the suitability of underground storage in sealed pits, a common feature of Iron Age sites.

Porch roof thatched with wheat straw

Massive porch based on an excavated plan of an actual Iron Age house

Industrial archeology

ARCHEOLOGY IS AS MUCH ABOUT TODAY – a lost key, a discarded plastic bag – as about the remote past. Over the last 300 years, there have been huge advances in making things – industrial archeology is the study of that technological change. Major industrial advances, like Abraham Darby's innovative use of coke to smelt iron (1709), are well known. But even the best-known industrial processes have unrecorded details, while much experimental work and many unspectacular industries have fallen into obscurity, from which archeology can rescue them. Trivial everyday details that fascinate us now were essential knowledge to the artisans of the time.

FLOATING TRANSPORT
Good communications are vital to industry, for bringing in raw materials and distributing finished products. Until railways revolutionized transportation in the mid-19th century, water was the only means of carrying low-value, bulky commodities. During the 1700s, canals were built to improve and extend the available water transport network.

GOING LIKE A ROCKET
Modern railways have their origins in wooden rails laid for moving heavy hand-drawn and horse-drawn wagons. By the late 1700s, there was a great need for reliable, all-season transportion. Stationary steam engines were becoming an important alternative to water power. Next in development was a steam powered moving engine to replace animal traction. In 1802, Richard Trevithick ran the first steam locomotive in the world.

George and Robert Stephensons' 1829 prizewinning *Rocket* locomotive was efficient and reliable, unlike its rivals

PIT WINDING GEAR
There was a great expansion in English coal mining during the 1600s. At later mines, like this one at Ironbridge, winding gear (operated by horse, then steam) brought coal to the surface. Archeological research has done much to reveal details of the early history of coal mining. Today it is hard to appreciate the dreadful conditions under which many miners worked.

Ironbridge Gorge's abundant natural resources (river transport, coal, iron ore, limestone, potter's clay, and water power) gave it a lead in the Industrial Revolution

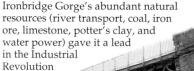

Huge, bottle-shaped kiln provided an updraft to keep temperature inside at 2282°F (1250°C)

CHINA WORKS
From the mid 1700s, several potteries in the Ironbridge Gorge, the center of the Industrial Revolution in England, began manufacturing imitations of expensive Chinese porcelain using china clay imported from southwestern England. Archeological work has documented the changing fortunes of these different potteries, providing much information on less prestigious local ceramics and the domestic lives of potters and other residents there.

THE IRON BRIDGE
The Severn River provided transport for industries developing on both sides of the Ironbridge Gorge, but it impeded local movement. The problem of bridging it was solved by building in iron. The world's first iron bridge, opened in 1781, was a splendid advertisement for the strength and versatility of cast iron – and an instant tourist sight. It made industry, especially ironworking, attractive to the layman and exciting to the entrepreneur.

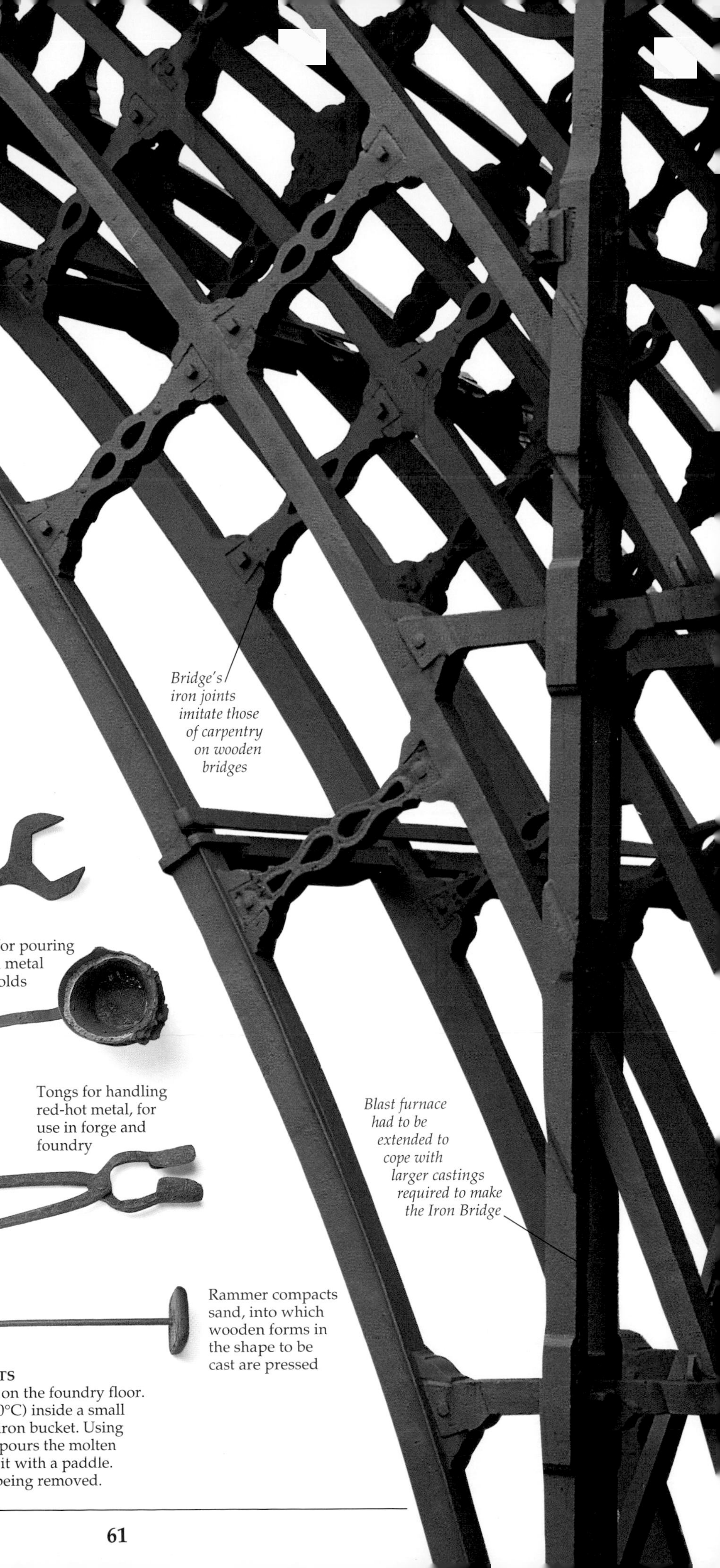

Pouring molten iron into sand mold

Padded gloves for protection

WHAT A BLAST!
Blast furnaces like Bedlam at Ironbridge produced "pigs" of cast iron, for casting or for working into wrought iron. The only remaining British producer of wrought iron is Ironbridge's Blists Hill. It operates as a living museum demonstrating many industrial, commercial, and domestic activities of the last century.

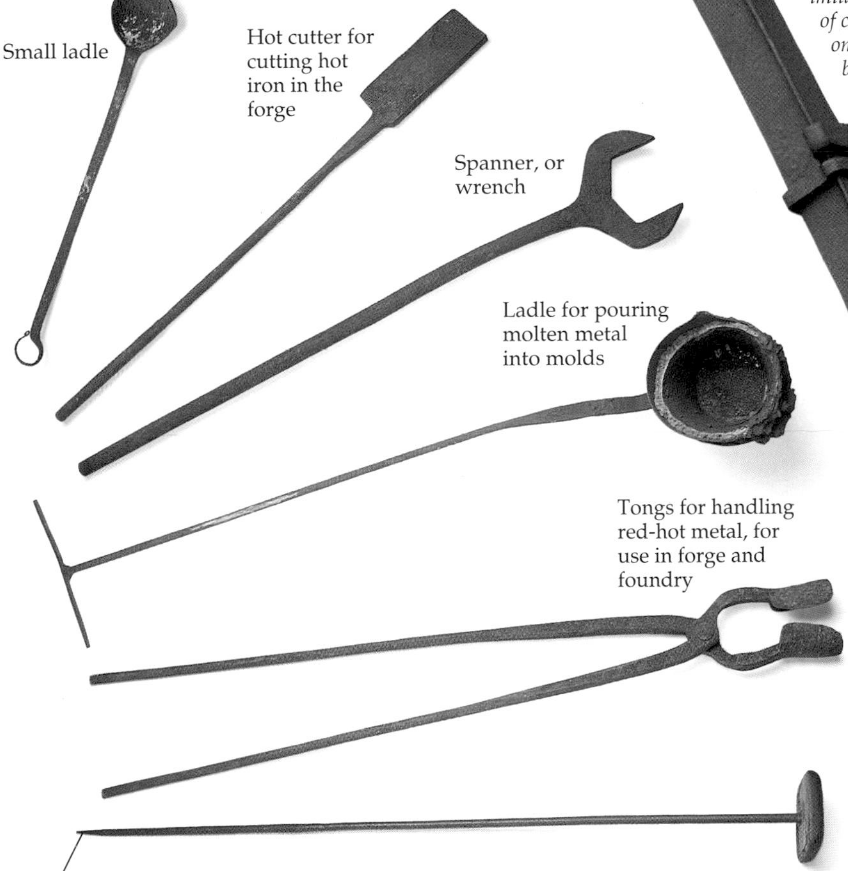

Bridge's iron joints imitate those of carpentry on wooden bridges

Small ladle

Hot cutter for cutting hot iron in the forge

Spanner, or wrench

Ladle for pouring molten metal into molds

Tongs for handling red-hot metal, for use in forge and foundry

Blast furnace had to be extended to cope with larger castings required to make the Iron Bridge

Spike for making holes in sand to release air as hot metal is poured into mold

Rammer compacts sand, into which wooden forms in the shape to be cast are pressed

CASTING IRON OBJECTS
Specially shaped molds are made in sand on the foundry floor. Pig iron is heated to about 2552°F (1400°C) inside a small furnace, releasing molten iron into an iron bucket. Using a long-handled ladle, the iron-maker pours the molten iron into the waiting molds, leveling it with a paddle. The castings are left to cool before being removed.

Past into future

W HY INVESTIGATE THE PAST? The past is not only a natural source of interest and wonder – it is also vitally important. At many levels, a knowledge of the past can help us today – for example, archeological work in such regions as Peru shows how some earlier farming methods can yield better, more sustainable results than modern ones. Knowing the past also gives people pride in their national identities. But the importance goes beyond this. The past, like the present, was created by individuals who acknowledged links at many levels – not only to their community but to humanity in general. The past belongs to everyone, uniting us in our human ancestry, giving us pride in our achievements as a species, and teaching us universal lessons. It is therefore essential that we ensure the survival of the relics of our past, threatened today as never before.

Vivid colours characterize Paleolithic paintings at Lascaux caves in southwestern France – having survived for over 12,000 years, many are now threatened

Mold growth, caused by visitors' breath upsetting environmental balance, damaged the paintings

HEADING FOR TROUBLE
Who owns the past – individual groups or everyone? In such areas as North America and Australia, the physical and cultural remains of native peoples' direct ancestors were plundered in earlier days. Often such cultural material has a living place in native traditions, and, quite rightly, much has been returned to their descendants. The question becomes more controversial as we go further back in time or deal with areas whose past involves many cultural groups. The issue is a sensitive one and arouses strong feelings.

Elaborate headdress

Bronze head from Benin in West Africa

Thin section of stone object as seen under a microscope

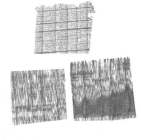

Slide showing anatomy of a beech tree including its tree rings

UNDER THE MICROSCOPE
Science today gives us many ways to investigate the past. Analyzing stone, pottery, or metal artifacts provides infor-mation on how they were made and where their raw materials came from. Scientific dating techniques are vitally important. Science also greatly helps con-serve and investigate organic materials, like human remains.

SLIVERS OF INFORMATION
Trees' annual growth rings give a calendar to date past wooden structures precisely. They also yield environmental information, since the width of tree rings relates to annual variations in temperature ar.d soil moisture. Archeology to-day investigates every aspect of the past and involves many other fields of srudy.

Running horse and other Lascaux paintings had to be protected, so caves have been closed to visitors

THE RUNAWAY PAST
Discovering the past may cause its destruction. Although excavation reveals artifacts from the past, it destroys their physical context except on paper, where reality is transformed into records (pp. 24–25). Much of the past survived because of unusual conditions, which discovery destroys. To prevent an object's decay, its conditions of preservation must be artificially maintained or recreated – for example, some of the wood from Somerset Levels has been redeposited in undrained peat in a nature reserve (pp. 46–47).

An exact replica of Lascaux's painted caves, including this horse, has been created for people to visit – a novel solution

ARCHEOLOGY AND THE PUBLIC
Fieldwalking and rescue excavation have always benefited enormously from the contribution of amateurs. Many archeological organizations now encourage public participation, especially by schoolchildren, in various activities such as experimental reconstruction. These children are building a kiln from wattle and daub.

CRUMBLING AWAY
Pollution is destroying our past and our future. Chemicals from industrial and domestic activities are badly damaging many structures that have stood for thousands of years. Car exhaust fumes are seriously corroding Greece's great monument, the Parthenon.

HERE TODAY, GONE TOMORROW
Relics of the past are being destroyed by roads, buildings, deep plowing, and massive peat cutting. In many countries laws protect the past, and require surveys, recording, and often rescue excavation before construction begins. While individual sites can be protected, ancient landscapes are slowly being destroyed by agriculture.

Excavator is rescuing vital information about Viking occupation

Rescue excavation at Roman and Viking York in England

Index

Acknowledgments

Dorling Kindersley would like to thank:

The British Museum, especially Ivor Kerslake for his efficient organization of the photography, and Peter Hayman, Chas Howson, Tony Milton, Nick Nicholls, Mike Row, and Trevor Springett for special photography; and for help on research Janet Ambers, Caroline Cartwright, Angela Evans, Dr. Anne Farrer, Loretta Hogan, Simon James, Janet Larkin, Dr. Andrew Oddy, Allyson Rae, Jeffrey Spencer, Judith Swaddling, Jonathan Tubb, David Williams, and Helen Wolfe.
For help on research and photography: Peter Reynolds, Copper Hastings, Edward Perry, Simon Harlow, and Dave Kirby at Butser Ancient Farm; Dr. Francis Pryor, Maisie Taylor, Janet Neve, Andy Dale, Toby Fox, and Bob

Woodward at Flag Fen Excavations; Kathy Tubb at The Institute of Archaeology (University of London); Dr. David de Haan, Katie Foster, and Marilyn Higson at The Ironbridge Gorge Museum; Dr. Margaret Rule, Andrew Elkerton, Alex Hildred, Richard Hubbard, Maggie Richards, and Sue James at The *Mary Rose* Trust; John Chase (photography), Gavin Morgan, Barry Gray, Jenny Hall, and Cheryl Thorogood at The Museum of London; Joslyn McDiarmid of Grosvenor Prints; and Mike Dunning, Lynton Gardiner, Colin Keates, Dave King, James Stephenson, Harry Taylor, and Michael Zabé for extra photography.
For design and editorial assistance: Sarah Cowley, Ivan Finnegan, Kati Poynor, Sharon Spencer, Helena Spiteri, Susan St. Louis, and Isaac Zamora.

Picture credits
t=top b=bottom c=center l-left r=right

Ancient Art & Architecture: 50bc, 53tr.
Archaeological Resource Centre: 63cr.
Bridgeman Art Library: 10tc.
British Museum: 14–15, 15c, 16cl, 16br, 17c, 20–21, 26cl, 26cr, 27br, 40bl, 40bc, 41cbr, 51b/Jonathan Tubb: 22cl, 22bl, 22bc, 23tc, 23tr, 23cr, 24tr, 24cr, 24b, 36c.
Bruce Coleman: 16bc/Nigel Blythe Photography: 18b/Trevor Barrett: 16tl/John Cancalosi: 16tr.
Comstock: 12bl.
C. M. Dixon: 30cl, 30tr, 31l, 31cr, 31br, 42bc.
Mary Evans: 11bc, 60tl.
E. T. Archive: 11br, 14b.
Flag Fen Trust: 37cr.
Jo Flood: 45ctr.
Werner Forman Archive: 29br, 53cl.
Kenneth Garrett: 13b, 42tl, 42cr, 43b.
Mike Gorman/Scott Polar Research Institute: 12cl.
Robert Harding Picture Library: 6–7b,
8cl, 62–63, 63cl.
Michael Holford: 21tl, 27tr, 57tr.
IBM/UK Ltd.: 53crt, 53crb.
INAH/Mexican Museum Authority 15b.
Mary Rose Trust: 6bl, 9br, 32tr, 33cl, 33cr, 34clt, 34clb, 34c, 34tr, 35r.
The Master and Fellows, Magdalene College, Cambridge: 32cl.
Museum of London: 9tr.
Novosti: 30br.
Roger Palmer: 12c, 12cr, 22br.
Axel Poignant Archive: 44bc.
Tom Rasmussen: 21cr.
Chris Scarre: 47cbr.
Science Museum 60ct.
Science Photo Library/Alfred Pasieka: 62br.
Suffolk County Council: 26tr.
Sutton Hoo Research Trust/Martin Carver: 43tr.
Dr. Martin Waller: 47b.
York Archaeological Trust: 6c, 10c, 46bl, 63b.
Michael Zabé 13t.